Real Belonging

GIVE SIBLINGS THEIR RIGHT TO REUNITE ®

LYNN S. PRICE

INKWATER PRESS

PORTLAND • OREGON

www.inkwaterpress.com

ISBN   1-59299-058-4

Publisher: Inkwater Press

Printed in the U.S.A.

This book is lovingly dedicated to:

Addison, Tanner and Jamie
for the privilege of being your mom

Andi
for the gift of being your sister

The youth of Camp To Belong, those I have fostered,
those I've been a CASA to, those I have mentored
and those who have chosen to call me Mom
for the honor of sharing your life journey

More praise for
REAL BELONGING

"Most of us accept the value of siblings as a given. Lynn Price does not. She found her only sibling after spending years in foster care. Since then she helped hundreds of disconnected siblings to reconnect. She also impacted child welfare agency services in many states and increased national awareness of this basic, but neglected, human need. This book is just one step in her unrelenting drive to fulfill some of children's deepest longings, and search for wholeness."

> —**Jake Terpstra,** *Child Welfare Services Specialist, (and) former Foster Care Specialist, U.S. Children's Bureau*

"In REAL BELONGING, Lynn Price uses equal parts of wit, wisdom, courage, and love to reveal the power of the sibling bond. She uses her personal experience to separate fact from fiction and deliver a unique insight into the foster care system. After a childhood of foster care starting at the age of 6 months, I celebrated my first birthday with my brothers at the age of 50. I have some advice for those of you who are either a parent or a guardian, a brother or a sister, or a professional providing for the welfare of children in need. Don't wait a half-century to learn about the magic and the power of real belonging, read the book!"

> —**Jerry Gitchel,** *foster child and proud brother of Lee and Tim Gitchel*

"Lynn Price is the real thing. She knows first hand about the power of belonging and has dedicated her life to bringing families together. Read this book and you'll feel compelled to buy a copy of REAL BELONGING for everyone you know."

> —**Mary LoVerde,** *author, "I Used to Have a Handle on Life but It Broke"*

"It's a story of hope, it's a story of courage, it's a story of inspiration and love. Who better to help us celebrate our cherished sibling relationships than the founder of Camp to Belong, Lynn Price, the biggest inspiration of all."

> —**Scott Friedman,** *President of the National Speakers Association, author of "Using Humor for a Change"*

"Camp To Belong was the best thing that could happen to anyone. I think that any person that is and wants to be a part of Lynn's wonderful dream will understand how each life is changed in response to the life that each child has been given and the ability to live again with the growth of their brothers and their sisters by their side."

> —**Darryl Weimer,** *former Camper*

"I've just seen a concept that I've never seen before, that makes such sense. Lynn Price is using senses in her visionary thinking. Once again it is breakthrough thinking which will revolutionize all visionaries."

> —**Juanell Teague,** *author of "The Zig Ziglar Difference"*

"Lynn Price provides distinctive insight into the special relationship among siblings. Don't lend this book to a friend...you're unlikely to get it back."

> —**Claudia A. Evart,** *Founder & President, Siblings Day Foundation*

"With a sensitivity born of her own sibling experience, Lynn Price has managed to underline and expand the sense of "family" and how that unit is strengthened with the joy of sibling celebration. This is a work which may well lubricate countless traditional families to welcome 'sibling foster care children' as whole units into their loving homes. It has noble purpose and will illuminate the reader's family insights."

—**Bob Danzig**, *former CEO Hearst Newspapers / author / speaker / foster child*

"As a foster/adoptive parent (first and foremost), I was forever changed when my daughters went to Camp To Belong with their brothers, who were living apart from us. From that first camp, I had a new awareness and commitment to making sure the four kids stayed connected...all the way to being able to become the adoptive parent and/or legal guardian to all four of them. As a social worker in the foster care system, the impact Lynn has made on me has been equally strong as I advocate for foster children. Lynn's passion, in REAL BELONGING, for some of the most vulnerable children in our society, is inspiring. The Camp To Belong "family" has been another family to my kids and it is easy for them to belong there."

—**Jennifer Lea Bronsdon,** *Social Worker, Foster Parent, Adoptive Parent and Legal Guardian*

Table of Contents

PART ONE

The Power of Real, My Story

PART TWO

The Passion of Belonging, Our Campers' Stories

PART THREE

The Power and Passion of Real Belonging

Foreword

I'll always remember that day in March of 1995. I drove from my house in Sycamore to O'Hare International Airport to spend an hour and a half with my sister. She had a lay-over and I will always take advantage of any moment I can spend with her. As we sat and talked, she asked what I thought about starting a camp for siblings that were separated through foster care. My immediate response was that I had never heard of it before but if she said it would happen, I knew it would. You see my sister lives her dreams and this I already knew about her.

Three months later, Camp To Belong, my sister's brainchild, hosted 32 campers in the state of Nevada. Fast forward to today, almost ten years later, Camp To Belong has given memories to over a thousand siblings and touched the hearts of countless others who have become part of the family or simply read about or heard the story.

Lynn has changed the world and I am so proud of all she has done. It really is quite amazing. But this is the professional side of my sister. I am privy to a very personal side of Lynn. Not only is she my sister, she is my dearest friend. I did not meet her until I was nine and she was eight. You will read about that in this book. We really did not start our relationship until we were young adults. Siblings across the United States, Canada and abroad will cherish childhood memories that Lynn and I never had, never will have, as you cannot turn back the hands of time. These children may have many things in life taken away from them but you can never take away the memories they have had at Camp To Belong with their brothers and sisters.

I have been asked what drove me to pursue my sister. My answer is, "I don't know." All I can imagine is that there is a magical bond that a sister has for her sister. It was like a light that drove me; I needed that relationship in my life. We were children, a time when you act on your emotions, not analyze them. I followed my emotions to Lynn. Today there is rarely a day that goes by that I do not hear her voice or read many e-mails from her. We leave each other messages just to connect or to say something to make each other laugh. We talk about our wonderful children, Camp To Belong, us and life in general. All walls are down when I talk or I'm with her. It is an incredible bond that now stands as an example to so many siblings. When the campers see us together, they have hope that if they are separated they can still have a wonderful bond with their brother or sister in their adult lives.

The world is a better place because of my sister Lynn. She is tiny in stature and gigantic in heart. Enjoy her story, learn from it and you too can catch the fever to be a better person and make our world that much better. On behalf of the Camp To Belong family I want to thank you Lynn for enriching all of us. I love you honey.

Andi Andree

Author's Note

Foster care was good for me.

Some say the "system" comes to us. In many cases such as mine, I came to the "system" at the decision of my family. Sure, the journey was unfortunate. There were twists and turns; no different from challenges experienced by other individuals and families.

However, somewhere along the way, I chose to look forward to give back. There was no option to be bitter. The option was only to be better. I surrounded myself with people who loved me unconditionally, supported me with sincerity and accepted me without judgment. These people inside and outside the "system" taught me what was real and showered me with a sense of belonging. My sister Andi, was and continues to be my beacon of real belonging.

I love the word "triumph." In fact, not too long ago when I coordinated a panel of former youth in care to speak about our triumphs, we marched into the room to the sound of trumpets. What happens in the "system" is real and we can be triumphant in securing belonging through the journey.

I share *Real* Belonging in three parts.

Part One, The Power of Real. My story weaves its way through my life in and beyond foster care.

Part Two, The Passion of Belonging. Our campers' stories celebrate the siblings of Camp To Belong, who demonstrate resiliency and purpose. They remind us that they, and their sibling connections, matter.

Part Three, The Power and Passion of Real Belonging. Honors my family in all the forms we have brilliantly taken.

Thank you for the privilege of sharing our stories. It is my hope that the words on these pages will encourage you to step up to the phone, take out a piece of stationery, or plan a trip (whether close or distant) to visit your own brothers and sisters. Remind them how significant they are in your life recalling memories shared together in childhood.

It is my hope that the next time your own children are squabbling and you send them to their separate rooms wondering why you became a parent, you will remember that sibling rivalry is a part of sibling connection.

It is my hope you will understand what is real and reach out to more youth in care with a sense of belonging as you foster and adopt sibling families.

There is a new definition of family. We know the importance of the parent-child relationship. Let's take a deeper look at brothers and sisters. Siblings are the longest relationships we most oftentimes have in life, surpassing the parent-child relationship.

It is vital we Give Siblings Their Right to Reunite®.

Sound the trumpets!

With humble appreciation,

Lynn Price

Did you know...

There are almost 600,000 children in foster care across the United States

65% - 85% have at least one sibling

30% have four siblings or more

75%, or 3 out of every 4, are separated from at least one sibling when placed in foster care

Statistics cited from Bernstein 2000, Phillips 1998, Hackman, Feathers-Acuna & Huston 1992, CASCW 2000 and Newberger 2001

This book is a true story about the genuine and generous people who have shared my life journey. In some cases, their names and places have been changed to protect the privacy of those involved.

PART ONE

The Power of Real, My Story

Name Calling

At eight years old, I was skipping home from school happier than I can ever remember. My ponytail was swinging side to side, my knees were kicking high, and the grin on my face spread from ear to ear. On this day, I'd escaped the wrath of the usual name calling and my heart was soaring. Way too often, by the time I'd made it to the schoolyard or classroom, someone was throwing out the first insult. "Bucky Beaver is back in town!" "Here comes Chicklets!" "Way to go, soon-to-be Tinsel Teeth!" I tried not to listen to their horrible words as the kids gawked at me. These two big, white protruding front teeth the size of Chicklets® gum glared from my mouth. The symbol of rejection, my teeth took on an iridescent glow whenever the sun hit them. Even as nighttime fell, they seemed to shimmer in the darkness.

This bright, sunny afternoon, I giggled, hoping that the kids at school were really starting to like me. While other girls played outside at recess and ate together at lunch, I usually stood alone in the corners of the playground or cafeteria, wishing they'd invite me to join them. On this day, I happily recalled an unexpected lunchtime invitation.

A group of girls called me to their table. I shivered with excitement as one of them shared her cookies with me. The rest of the afternoon, my hand bolted up in confidence in each class. I felt it was my smart day to answer questions and soak in the response any kid wants to hear: "Good answer, Lynn." I started thinking about which new friend to invite over for the weekend, imagining the fun of playing games and making up dances to the beat of our favorite music.

I'd spent my days at school trying desperately to position my top gums whichever way I could to hide the monsters. I would rarely speak and when I did, my mouth hardly opened. I trembled, anticipating the mean ridicule about to come my way - an unavoidable race to see which of the know-it-all kids would lead the parade of name calling.

I can see myself so clearly on the playground at Middleton Elementary School in Skokie, Illinois. I'd choose to play "four squares" so the kids would look at the big, orange rubber ball we tossed back and forth, rather than focus on me. I'd hop on the first available swing and kick pump so high, only opening my mouth when I sprung all the way forward and up. Then the kids could only see the dirty bottoms of my penny loafers. Sometimes I'd play tetherball and wish the ball on the string would come around fast enough to knock my teeth out. Alas, it was only a matter of time before I'd get caught off balance in a field game and my enormous teeth made their ghastly appearance.

By contrast, at the end of each day, I couldn't wait to see Mom and feel the safety of my home. On Kimball Street, I'd enjoyed the life of an only child until age seven. That's when Mom and Dad adopted my baby brother, Jeff. During his first year, I loved being his big sister. When he'd smile at me, I'd openly smile back with all my teeth showing. He only giggled. Nothing that resembled meanness or an insult ever came from his little body.

After homework on each school day, I'd venture into the neighborhood playing with Lassie, the full-size collie in the yard next door. During early evening, my best friend Lane would cross the street and knock at my door. We'd call on the other kids up and down the block to play hide and seek, have squirt gun fights, or play baseball at the corner where we used the round street sewer covers as bases.

The kids on Kimball were nice to me. Lane was like my big brother. Only a year and half older than me, he lived in the same type of duplex on the other side of the street. Our moms were best friends and our families spent a lot of time together. Both oldest in our families, we were responsible for many family chores. We always took our roles in stride, supporting each other along the way. When he'd show up at my door, I felt the safety of an unspoken bond on the other side. Lane had always looked out for me, helping me finish my chores and homework so we could draw our neighborhood friends near and team up in happiness at being out of school. Lane taught me how to ride a bike. Our biggest claim to fame was building a 42 deck card house. Everyone had to tiptoe around the house for days.

Each evening, I'd look forward to see Dad's car come around the corner about 6:30. I'd run toward him with arms held out and a big hug. His arrival always meant the end of play and the start of dinner. As we'd walk inside the house together, I'd turn to my friends and wave to Lane, meeting his eyes with thanks for another wonderful day as my big brother and friend.

Dad would wash up from the grind of his glacier shop. He'd grown up in Hungary and had a blessed pride in both coming to America and owning his own business. The glass and mirrors he measured, sanded, cleaned and delivered reflected his confidence in making a living and taking care of his family.

Dad would join Mom, Jeff and me at the dinner table. It felt good being at home embraced by a loving family and a home-cooked meal. Then, I'd go off to Hebrew school for an evening of religious lessons followed by mint chocolate chip ice cream – always in a dish – from Baskin Robbins before it was time to go to bed.

That serenity and stability changed the afternoon I was skipping home in 1963. I didn't realize how simple my life had been. Oh, how I came to prefer the "Bucky Beaver," "Chicklets" and "Tinsel Teeth" comments. My unending quest to hide my teeth and avoid the name calling was nothing compared to how I'd have to hide my life.

That sunny and bright day, it was as if the kids actually knew what lie ahead of me. No one called me a name. They let me be at the lunchroom table and the answer expert in class.

When the end-of-day bell rang, I skipped out the door, smiling big and giggling with delight. I played hopscotch on the imaginary grid chalked in front of me being sure to hop right, jump with both feet, hop left and end at the big number ten, known as "sky blue." I took a penny out of my penny loafer and tossed it from line to line with a double clap when it landed smack dab in the middle of the crack. Then I switched to avoid stepping on a crack in the sidewalk. The words to the game lingered in my mind: *Don't step on a crack because you'll break your mother's back.*

As I approached my home, it was as if I'd landed on the crack. I stopped abruptly when I saw Dad's car parked in front of the house. I shuddered. Dad never came home early. *Was he sick? What was terribly wrong? What could be happening inside?* My mind exploded with different thoughts and my eyes raced from the gold station wagon to the front door. *Why was he home early?*

I crept across the lawn and up the front stoop, pulling the outside silver screen door slowly to avoid its familiar squeak. I was surprised to see the heavy walnut door pushed open on the inside. I prayed I wouldn't be noticed as I tiptoed into the front entry, turning back toward the door to close it ever so quietly.

I caught a glimpse of the station wagon once again and hoped that everything was okay. Bad news made my stomach hurt. I didn't want to hear it. I hoped it wasn't about me. The silence was deafening.

As I turned around, I was startled to see Mom and Dad sitting motionless on the kelly green couch to my right. I glanced to the left in fright, only to see the lines in their foreheads reflected in the arched, smoky mirrors that Dad had crafted above and around the picture windows. Both of their faces were drawn at the temples and blown to contortions at their cheekbones. Their hands reached for each other in unison. The back of my neck got cold; perspiration wet my forehead and underarms. My heart beat wildly. I wanted to run, but my feet wouldn't move. Mom and Dad met my questioning eyes with blank stares. Their silence seemed to last forever.

Real Secrets

How was your day at school?" Mom asked, breaking the eternal silence.

As I whispered, "Just fine," I anticipated something much more important would follow that question. I continued to stand in the entry way, shifting my weight from side to side. My eyes darted to the plastic that covered the couch and the beautiful religious pictures spotlighted on the wall above. I could hear Jeff giggling in the back room. It was the perfect family image with everyone in their place - except for Mom and Dad's faces and clenched hands. In an instant I would feel out of place.

I could only avoid eye contact with them for so long. When I finally mustered the courage, I looked at Dad's eyes and saw a deep sadness through his tears. "Honey," he stammered, "we have something to tell you. We've been wanting to share this information for some time, but the moment just never seemed right." I wondered, *What is so right about now?*

As he searched for words, my legs started to move on their own and I stumbled forward. Almost losing my balance, I sank down on the edge of the couch next to Mom and Dad. My body shook uncontrollably.

"Where do I start?" Dad coughed to clear his voice. "Well, you see, umm, how do I say this?" He said one word, but didn't finish a sentence. He paused with his eyes recklessly peering toward Mom, the wall, his feet and me. And my eyes followed every move his eyes made. My schoolbooks fell off my lap as I reached for their entwined hands. Feeling uneasy, I retracted them quickly and rubbed my sweaty palms together.

Dad followed a long pause with, "We are not your parents. We..."

I jumped to my feet, "Mom, oh my gosh, tell him to stop!" My head swirled until I felt dizzy. My knees buckled. I fell back on the couch and my head struck the cushion. I closed my eyes. I opened my eyes. I could only look straight ahead. Fright showed on all of our faces in the smoky mirrors across the room.

Mom continued with a strained but firm tone. "Lynn, we are not your real parents. We are your foster parents." Mom's words were always more direct than Dad's. In our family, Mom always delivered the tough messages.

"Foster parents. What does that mean?" I asked as I backed up toward the single blue wicker chair that stood clear across the room near the mirrors. Tears stung my eyes. I sank into the lonely chair and my hands shook. I probed the surface of the chair, sticking my fingers into the holes that filled the wicker back, like I was trying to stop a dam from overflowing.

What did I do to deserve this? I threw my hands up in the air and then hugged myself, feeling so alone on that side of the room. I wanted to run back across and hug them. I wanted to punch them. I wanted to scream, but my vocal chords couldn't even give a whisper. I glared at the mosaic grid of wicker flashing to the sun's reflection in the plastic of the couch where Mom and Dad sat.

All I ever knew was ripped away. I desperately wanted to feel their closeness, but I couldn't even feel my own body. I went over their words in my head wishing I had heard them incorrectly. I'd always been Daddy's little girl. Now he told me he's not my daddy. *How could this happen? What did I do to cause this heart-wrenching situation?*

"But, you are my parents," I cried in protest. "Why are you making up this story?"

With swollen eyes, Dad continued, "Your real father abandoned you."

I listened to his words but it seemed like he was telling me a fairy tale. "We heard he was a bad man, a ladies man and a gambler. Your mother suffered a nervous breakdown when he left. He took the car and their money, and set out without you. You were just eight months old when your mother entered a mental institution. She was very ill. They say she was heartbroken when your father left."

I was sure this made-up story came from a book or a TV show. It was certainly not from my life. *Did I dare turn the next page? Could I turn off the TV or change the channel?* His voice droned on and a huge lump overtook my throat. I sobbed wildly. Just when I thought I couldn't stand another word, Dad continued, "At that time, there was no one in your family to take care of you and your sister."

"What! But, I don't have a sister! I have a brother!" I shouted. "What family? *You* are my family!" I screamed.

"Well, you do have a sister across town," Mom explained with a sigh. "Her name is Andre. She's a year and a half older than you and she lives with a different foster family. We weren't allowed to take both of you."

Suddenly, they were rushing to release the burden of carrying this heavy secret. Mom spoke rapidly. "Your *real* Mom is no longer in the hospital. She wants to meet you and your *real* sister. She may want to take you back."

"Take me back? What does that mean?!" I stuttered, hardly breathing. I wondered if I could ever look to Mom and Dad for trust and support again. They weren't my parents. I had a *real* mother who wanted to take me back. I was the *big* sister. Now they were telling me I was the *little* sister. Jeff wasn't my brother. I might have to go back. *To where?*

I had never heard the words "foster parents" before. I certainly didn't want to meet another mother or a new sister. My head kept pounding deeper with the unanswered question, *Take me back to where?* I couldn't *stand* another moment with them.

I ran to my room and jumped on my bed, throwing the covers over me. I hugged my favorite doll Queenie and cried out loud, kicking my feet. Now the kids at school would really tease me. I imagined their cruel words shouting in my head. "Here comes Bucky Beaver with no *real* parents."

My life as I knew it just vanished. I, Lynn Schreiber, had been cut like an umbilical cord from what I had always known. My mom, dad and brother weren't *really* my family. I had a *real* mother. I had a *real* sister.

Secrets were unveiled. Feeling uncomfortable in my own body, I shook at the thought of living these secrets.

Queenie

Hi Queenie,

It was a terrible day. I hope you are still mine. I found out today that Mom and Dad *really* aren't "my parents." I don't get it. I am so sad and want to run away from this terrible and confusing stuff. I'll take you with me, I promise. I don't believe this. I want to ask questions but I'm scared. When I think about all of this, I get a big lump in my throat and my stomach hurts. My head moves from side to side. I don't know if I should run to them or turn around and run away.

Can you tell me what to do?

I keep thinking about me. But what are Mom and Dad thinking? Should I think about Mom and Dad? Should I think about my *real* mother and *real* sister? I want to know everything, but I really don't want to know anything. What does *real* mean anyway?

Thinking about my *real* mother and *real* sister is driving me crazy. Why did everyone keep secrets about me? What are they hiding? I feel so different now.

I am so scared about meeting my *real* mother and *real* sister. If so many secrets are being told now, how many more will they tell me? Who can I trust?

What does my *real* mother look like? What will happen to Mom and Dad? How can I be the little sister when I've always been the big sister? What does "foster" mean?

I try to think of my life without Mom, Dad and Jeff. I try to think of my life with my *real* mother and *real* sister, who are strangers. I thought I belonged here. But now I might have to go there. How come I didn't know anything?

I am so angry. My parents are MINE. I *am* the big sister. I love my baby brother. We are family.

I want to be strong, but I am so confused. I feel like a little baby. I want to cry and be cuddled. I want them to tell me everything. I don't want to have to ask.

Are they keeping more things from me? Is it my fault that I'm not asking questions?

Did I do something wrong for this to happen? Am I being punished? I am hurting so bad. I don't want Mom and Dad to hurt, too.

I don't want anyone to feel sorry for me, but I'm feeling sorry for myself.

Mom and Dad said they didn't want others to know this secret. Right now, I don't want to talk to anyone else because I don't know what to say. They would have questions. I don't have answers. But I can talk to you, Queenie, even though they said I couldn't tell anyone. They said no one else knew. They said we have a family secret now. Nobody needed to know. Are they embarrassed? Did they do something wrong?

The truth is I don't belong to them. Mom and Dad aren't my mom and dad.

Help me, Queenie.

The Drive

Only yesterday I heard the *real* secret. Today I would live it.

The dawn brought a sunny spring morning through the red rose-covered curtains in my bedroom. I couldn't sleep, yet I kept the blanket and quilt over my head to pretend I was sleeping if Mom or Dad walked in. I tossed and turned all night, having nightmares even while I was awake. I just couldn't believe the news that Mom and Dad weren't Mom and Dad. I used my pinkie to fold back the top cover so I could glance at my alarm clock. I wished it would get stuck in an early time position. I knew any moment the door would open. Instead of getting ready for school, I'd be getting ready for The Visit. Mom had already laid out clothes she called "special for the day." I knew nothing was going to be special about this day. It was sunny outside, but inside, my mood remained cloudy.

I heard the bedroom door open and felt the covers being pulled back. Dad brushed his hand across my forehead and whispered softly, "Time to get up, honey." His voice calmed me. I turned around and looked into his sullen eyes, his bags showing beneath the rims. As he walked out of the room, I scooted off the bed. A numbness washed over me and I wished it would drown out my nervousness. The anticipation of learning a past I didn't know about caused me to grab the pillow and hold it to my face. I put on the "special clothes." Once dressed, I peered into the mirror wondering if I'd see the same person I saw yesterday.

I gave Queenie a hug before I left the room. Dad walked out of the house first. Mom, staring into nowhere, followed him. He looked my way and gave me a wink. Dad always tried to make me feel good. Our connection lingered until he opened the back car door. I watched his hand shake as he pushed down the lock after I got in. He closed the door and walked around to his side. Mom got into the front seat in silence and we all turned toward the front door of the house at the same time. *What would life look like when we walked back through it?* We didn't speak about what was going to happen at The Visit. We didn't even speak about what would happen *after* The Visit.

Everything that had seemed safe disappeared out our car windows as we drove down our street. The scenes on the outside showed signs of the renewal of spring in its warmth and beauty. The view in my mind filled with ugly thoughts of change. I shivered.

I used to love these drives, just Mom, Dad, Jeff and me. I knew Jeff was too young to even understand what was happening on this day. As I thought about not being his big sister, a tear ran down my cheek. I hated everything; this car, this family, this day. I left Queenie behind thinking I'd be strong and courageous, but now I wished she were in my arms to catch my tears.

As we drove, I looked out and focused on the park that had my very favorite swing. I loved going there with Dad. He would push me on my swing until I thought I'd go over the top. Even when my own pumping took me higher, I asked Dad to push me so I could feel his strong hands on my back. We laughed out loud as he ran underneath and I soared up to the sky, only to swing backwards and look into his eyes with delight.

We approached the edge of our small city and turned on to Greenbay and Sheridan Roads, lined with beautiful trees framing a magnificent view of the B'hai Temple. The dome took up the sky with its golden crown and its splendor invited calmness. I wondered if Dad chose the scenic route to delay us getting to The Visit. I thought it was cool that Dad didn't want to get there any faster than I did. Then I was jolted back to what I had learned the day before. *He's not my dad! So why would he care which way he goes?*

Gazing at the Northwestern University campus, I thought about what I wanted to be when I grew up. I knew that's where kids went when they were old enough to leave their own moms and dads - a proud moment of moving on. But I was about to leave my mom and dad at eight years old! I didn't feel any pride. I wondered if they were proud.

In this moment, I suddenly realized I couldn't wait to leave these people who were not my mom and dad. I wanted to go anywhere. I didn't care what I wanted to be. I just wanted to go and leave all the secrets behind.

As we drove out of the suburbs, I escaped into memories that loosened my clenched jaw and fisted hands. I marveled at Lake Shore Drive with its splendid beaches on one side and Gold Coast buildings on the other. I watched waves lap up on the beach and saw birds soar over the water, landing on its sandy edge.

On the beach, people walked briskly, sometimes timing their steps to miss the waves and being sure not to touch the cold water with their feet. Across the street, people carried their briefcases and grocery bags as they headed home or to work.

Arriving at the edge of downtown, Mom broke the silence. "That's the Drake Hotel," she said pointing toward the tall building in front of us. She explained, as she did every time, that was where she and Dad spent their wedding night.

"I know," I responded quietly, going back into my own thoughts.

Actually, I was more interested in the Water Tower and recalled the story about Mrs. O'Leary and her cow making history. I stared at Marina Towers, those twin round buildings, and wondered if people got dizzy walking in circles inside it.

Amid the safety of my own thoughts, I wondered where all the people out there were going. *Were any of them looking for their mom? Could one of them be mine?* I shuddered and lost myself again, counting the people walking, studying license plates and finding objects that started with each letter of the alphabet.

I clearly wanted to avoid the two people in the front seat. I wanted to talk, but the words wouldn't come out of my mouth. I wanted to say, *I love you Mom and Dad,* but all of a sudden they were strangers. After all, they told me they weren't my mom and dad; they were my "foster parents." I still didn't know what that meant.

I recalled my Bucky Beaver challenge. *What would my friends think of me now? What kind of story could I tell them?* And I figured I'd really have to make up a whopper of an excuse for missing school.

But making up a story couldn't get me out of The Visit. There was so much I didn't know, so I didn't even know what to ask. I didn't know how I was going to talk to this *real* mother.

Mom and Dad have always been *real* to me. Now, Mom and Dad are my foster parents. But I'd never call them "foster." I was so confused.

Mom stopped her sightseeing tour and Dad focused on the road. Way before I was ready, we arrived for The Visit.

The Visit

Our car pulled into a parking garage just off Michigan Avenue. Dad slowly rolled down his window and stuck his hand out to take the ticket. He drove up and around level after level to find an open space. With each turn, I hoped for another row of filled spaces.

Our eyes met in the rear view mirror. His lips quivered and pursed as if to talk, but no words came out. I was getting dizzy as the car turned in circles. I was also getting dizzy thinking about what Dad wanted to say and what The Visit would be like.

We got out of the car in silence and Dad motioned us to the elevator at the far end of the garage. I used to love pressing the elevator button, but now I didn't want to go near the button or the elevator. I looked around at the car, wishing we could run back and drive far away.

Mom pressed the down button. The elevator bell rang and the doors opened. While she pressed another button inside, I walked into Dad's arms, burying my head in his stomach with my chin resting on his belt. Both of us trembled. His hands hugged my back tightly.

We walked out of the elevator toward the street and around to the front of the high rise building. I focused on the sign outside, "Jewish Children's Bureau." I didn't know what bureau meant, but I did know The Visit at the bureau would change our lives.

I walked feebly through the lobby dragging my feet with my head down. The gray walls and chrome furniture matched my sickly feeling. If it was a place for children, why didn't I hear any laughter? Do all children come here to find their *real* mothers? Is this really the mental hospital my mother comes from? *I want to go home!*

We stepped inside an office and Mom walked up to the receptionist. "I'm Jackie Schreiber. We are here to see the social worker." Dad gently motioned me to the chair in the empty waiting room. In a few minutes, I heard a female voice say, "How are you, Jackie?" She appeared from nowhere. I didn't notice her approaching us. Without waiting for an answer, she flexed her index finger for us to follow her to a room at the far end of a dark hall. I guessed the woman was a social worker, but she didn't tell us her name. She only wanted to know how my mom was.

Again, the woman asked, "How are you doing, Jackie?" I wondered why my mom wasn't responding to her. *For gosh sakes, answer her and let's get out of here!*

The woman's voice bounced around the starkness of the room. No windows or pictures on the walls. No plants. No coloring books. It smelled stale. I paced slowly around the room avoiding a chair. I couldn't sit still, so I leaned against the wall and ran my fingertips across the barren desk.

I kept my eyes on the door as the woman closed it. She looked directly at me and spoke for the third time, "Jackie, has the cat got your tongue?"

I looked at Mom. *Why isn't she answering?*

She turned to me and whispered, "That's you." I locked my arms together in an effort to be bold. My mouth became dry. I froze like a statue. *How could I be Jackie?*

"But Mom, *you* are Jackie," I whispered back. I groped for reassurance by looking at Dad. His eyes shot in another direction. Mom shook her head from right to left. I wasn't sure if I should stay silent or scream at the top of my lungs.

"But Mom, my name is Lynn. You know that!" My face fell into my palms. I jerked my head up quickly. Through clenched teeth and eyes shifting from the woman to Mom and Dad, I proclaimed, "My name is Lynn!"

Mom gently took my arms, turned me toward her and said, "The truth is, your *real* name is Jackie Lynn Paul." She glanced at the woman and gestured for her to continue the conversation, but the woman didn't speak.

Mom patiently looked back at me and explained, "You see, in the Jewish religion, mothers and daughters can't share the same first name. So your Dad and I call you Lynn. Lynn is really your middle name. Jackie is your first name. Schreiber is our last name."

I looked at Dad. He stood by the corner in the shadows of the gloominess that enveloped the room. He didn't say anything and he wouldn't look at me.

I stared blankly at the woman, realizing I hadn't answered her question about how I was doing. All the pain, all the confusion and all the unanswered questions poured from my eyes. I cried. I was in the middle of a storm, with a tidal wave coming over my body and raindrops turning to hail. I sobbed, shook and cried out, yet no one came near. I backed away from Mom and Dad toward the door. I felt all alone.

Then, there was a quick knock at the door. It opened slowly. Through my bloodshot eyes, I looked curiously at the woman who stood in the doorway. She entered the room. She had a look of sadness in her eyes, yet a crooked smile shaped her lips. I just wanted to run past her and bolt to the other side of the door. I couldn't stand another moment of secrets being revealed. *What's next?*

"Jackie, this is your mother," said the social worker. I first looked at my parents and felt a total sense of loss consume my body. I reluctantly turned my attention to the woman introduced as my mother. I stood motionless. I memorized her small stature, her bouffant hairdo and bright blood-red lipstick as she continued to stare at me.

Standing next to her was a curly haired girl only a little taller than me. In the heavy silence of that moment, I was paralyzed.

"Hi, Jackie," said my *real* mother. Her soft voice startled me as I backed up and hit the wall behind me. My eyes darted from Mom to this *real* mother. "I thought about you so much and have missed you desperately," she said in a quiet voice. My gaze turned to the girl beside her, but my mind instantly shut her out. I shouted, "She's not my sister. She's not my sister!"

Facing Backwards

I don't even remember saying good-bye to my *real* mother and *real* sister. I don't remember getting back on the elevator. I don't remember walking to the car. All I could hear were our footsteps on the pavement and the keys dangling in Dad's hands. Mom and Dad remained silent. I didn't know what to say. We didn't even look at each other.

Is everything going to be okay? Why didn't Mom and Dad tell me everything would be okay?

I didn't know if I acted right. Everything was a blur. A dazed walk. A sickly gray and chrome. A social worker. A new name. A *real* mother with red lipstick. A *real* sister with curly hair. Mercifully, The Visit was over.

I wanted to tell Mom and Dad I loved them, but I didn't know if I should anymore. I didn't know how to talk to them about my *real* mother and *real* sister.

When we got to the car, I walked to the passenger door behind the driver. Opening it, I set one foot in the car and abruptly pulled it out. I slammed the door shut, turned and marched to the back, pulling open the latch of the station wagon door. I climbed into the seat that faced backwards, looking out at my past behind me instead of looking forward at Mom and Dad and my uncertain future.

I wanted to be far away from them. I didn't want to look at their faces. I didn't want to see Dad's eyes in the mirror. I felt empty in their company. I didn't belong.

When I stopped thinking of me though, I felt sorry for them. They had kept a secret from me and from everyone. I wanted to punch the seats. I wanted them to be the first to speak. How I wished they'd explain why they didn't tell me sooner. I searched for words to say in the car and hoped Dad would pull the car over to the side of the road. We needed to fill the space with answers to questions.

As much as I wanted to be quiet and far away, I also wanted to climb into the front seat between them. I remember I used to sit between them on important days. This definitely would rank up there as an important day. I wanted to stretch to the front and remind them I was still in the car. They had always taken such good care of me; they had always loved me. I had everything a little girl could want, including a beautiful room, new clothes and toys. Now I felt like I had nothing. I felt so alone. I needed my parents. I wondered if they needed me.

I fumbled for thoughts about what had just happened during The Visit. I couldn't believe I walked into a room and was introduced to my *real* past and a future new life. My first name wasn't Lynn; my *real* name was Jackie. My last name wasn't Schreiber; it was *really* Paul. Jackie Lynn Paul. They changed my name! For me, or for them? Perhaps they worried about what people would think. Perhaps they were trying to protect something. I wanted everything to be out in the open. They continued to want to keep the secrets.

I groped to find words to talk about my *real* mother with Mom sitting in the front seat. I shook as I thought about my *real* sister. What about my brother, Jeff? Would he let me hug him when we got home? How would he feel about having a new sister? But the sister wasn't his! Gee whiz, was Jeff *really* my brother?

I put my fingers to the sides of my forehead and pressed, cross-eyed in thought. I threw my shoulders back to stretch the kinks that consumed my body. *My mom or my real mother? What about Dad? Would I cuddle Jeff again? How could I be a friend with this new girl? Who else knew about MY life?*

However, I knew that the mint chocolate chip ice cream would make me feel better and I hoped Dad would stop at Baskin Robbins on the way home. I just knew that when we got inside our door, he would pick me up and whirl me around. I just knew we would sit around the kitchen table and they would talk to me. Maybe it would not be a big deal and everything would be okay. We all just needed time.

But Dad passed my favorite ice cream store and the chocolate mint chip ice cream. As he turned down our street, I saw the kids playing at the baseball sewers. The pitcher was getting ready to throw the ball. I ducked down and hid on the floor. I knew they would ask where I was all day. I didn't want them to hate me. No other kid in the neighborhood lived with parents who weren't *really* their parents! I knew they wouldn't understand. Well, I didn't understand so how could they? I wondered if Lane would still be my friend.

I ran up the front steps of the house and hid between the screen door and the regular door until Mom turned the key in the lock. I pushed the door open and ran into the kitchen so no one could see me through the front windows. I waited for Mom and Dad to follow me so we could talk at last. I waited and waited. They never came.

Everything was not going to be okay.

What did I do wrong? I crept up to the living room on my hands and knees, stretching my ear toward the turn in the hall. Mom and Dad were whispering. I couldn't make out a word. I laid my head in my hands. I trembled thinking my *real* mother would take me away. I wondered what my *real* sister was thinking. Was she going through the same thing? Maybe she just found out about her *real* mother and her *real* sister, too.

Mostly, I wanted my life to go backwards.

Interviews

During the weeks that followed The Visit, I didn't dare talk to Mom and Dad about that day. When the kids at school and in my neighborhood asked where I had been, I changed the subject. I felt helpless and hopeless.

My head and heart were sending me different messages. My mind skipped from absolute confusion to concrete denial. I just didn't understand what was happening. A new kind of silence took over our home. While Jeff giggled on the outside, I cried on the inside. I didn't want anything to change between my parents and me, but anticipating a change caused me to build walls of separation.

I wanted to understand why strangers had control of me. I had never met the people from the social service system who were sharing information and making decisions about my life. Although I learned they were social workers and knew things about me, I knew nothing about them. They talked about me and didn't ask how I felt, whether I had questions or if I even cared. I couldn't believe anything or anyone. I didn't know what to do. I kept reminding myself that Mom and Dad told me to keep everything secret.

In this nightmare of a life, I banged my head against the wall trying to rid myself of the distrust I felt toward the people

I had never questioned before. I couldn't imagine leaving Mom and Dad because I'd always felt safe and loved with them. I really wanted to know that everything was going to be all right.

Shortly after The Visit, monthly get-togethers were scheduled with my *real* mother. Each time, we were supervised by a social worker. Sometimes the social worker asked questions to my *real* mother and me, and other times, she just took notes watching and listening. Frankly, I could barely look at this *real* mother. I squirmed in my seat, having nothing much to say at all.

"Bernyce is your mother," the social worker told me one day before she arrived. "She loves you very much."

"I don't even know her," I responded.

I couldn't bear to think about her as Mother. Even Mom. Mommy was out of the question. I already had a Mom, a Mother and a Mommy. "My mom's name is Jackie," I adamantly told everyone. "Whoever *she* is," turning my head toward the stranger, "she isn't my mother!"

I wouldn't call her Bernyce, either. If I needed to say something, I just spoke in her direction and hoped she would listen. But most times, she was asking questions. She had an agenda. She had the notepad poised for my responses. She asked and I answered with as few words as possible. It was a constant interview with a stranger, and I hated it.

During these get-togethers we didn't go to the playground, we didn't have ice cream, we didn't go to the movies. We sat in a cold stark room or a booth in some restaurant. No matter how many questions I had, I never asked them. I felt like I was on the nightly news reporting on my life, answering a barrage of her questions. *Why did she even care?* I dreaded the day all my friends would see me on TV. Then my world would really turn upside down. Bucky Beaver didn't sound so bad anymore. I couldn't imagine what the kids would call me when they heard all this. I wondered if they would ever play with me again, especially since I was keeping a distance. They would have all kinds of questions, and I still didn't have any answers. I yelled at myself because I didn't have the nerve to ask my *real* mother questions.

It felt really strange that a social worker, who was also like a stranger, always watched over my *real* mother and me. I worried that I had done something wrong. Later, I learned the social worker had to be with us so she could record how we acted together for our files.

Mom and Dad finally talked to me about the social worker. They said it was her job to make sure I was safe and happy. She was supposed to listen to the questions my *real* mother asked and make sure I answered only those I felt comfortable with. The social worker would help decide if my *real* mother could take me back along with my *real* sister. I made sure to always tell the social worker I was just fine where I was. I told her I loved my parents.

Sometimes my *real* mother's sister, Evelyn, came too. Her sad eyes looked back and forth between my *real* mother and me. She told me how much my *real* mother loved and missed my *real* sister and me. She would talk about getting together soon again. I wondered if she wanted to grab both of us and run.

Sometimes my *real* sister Andre came to these get-togethers. One thing was very clear; our *real* mother was in charge.

Mom and Dad or a social worker would take me to see Andre and our *real* mother month after month. We'd meet outside a restaurant. Each time, my *real* mother looked me up and down from a distance, cocking her head with a sad, soft smile. Her opening words were usually something like, "You're so skinny," or "How are you, honey?" I cringed. *Why did she call me honey? Was being skinny bad?* I whispered back to her, "Hello." Andre and I never had much to say to each other.

We went to the same restaurant often. It must have been downtown because we took Sheridan Road to get there. I still remember the deli with its shiny counters and chrome. I played a jukebox that had individual selectors at each table to distract me. My *real* mother smooshed me into the booth as if to say, "You're not going anywhere now." If the social worker came, she sat on the other side of the table. If Andre came, she put the three of us on one side and she sat in the middle. She made sure Andre, who was placed on the outside, was boxed in by her purse. I peeked under the table to see if there was enough room to climb out. There never was.

I looked through the song selections and sang the songs in my head so I wouldn't have to listen to her or answer questions. I started playing with the top of the sugar container, the kind with a little silver spout on top. I saw other people in the restaurant, but they seemed so distant. I wanted one of the people to come and rescue me. *Didn't they know I was with strangers?*

I ordered the same thing every time. Hot beef with mashed potatoes and gravy. I tried to show her I do eat - and eat big. And another reason: I could hardly look her in the eye. I very badly wanted my mind to wander to other things instead of the topics at hand, so I focused on eating. I took a bite of meat alone, then potatoes alone and then bread alone. Then I ate the meat with the potatoes and the meat with the bread. Then I ate the bread with the potatoes and then all three together. After each circle of the plate, I started all over again.

My *real* mother would say, "You never know, you may want to come back to me."

I didn't know what I was supposed to know. But she knew what she needed. At each visit, she literally had her notepad at all times. She acted like a secretary. I spoke and she asked me to slow down. As she questioned me about my life, she asked me to spell things out, like the name of my school, my friend's names and more. I spelled for her "M-I-D-D-L-E-T-O-N" for my school or "D-A-R-L-E-N-E" for my friend. I told her Darlene and I loved baking cookies together. "What is your teacher's name, honey?" she'd ask. I was afraid to answer. I wondered if she was going to call her and talk about me. I reluctantly said, "Miss Kurzweg." "Spell it," she said. "K-U-R-Z-W-E-G." She asked me how I spent my summers. I told her, "With my friend S-H-E-L-L-E-Y at Roger's Park day camp." I told her Shelley and I received medals for being the best campers together. I also shared that Lane and I spent weeks of the summer with our families at a cottage on the beaches of M-I-C-H-I-A-N-A.

When Andre was with us, our *real* mother asked her questions too. Andre and I never seemed to talk much to each other. When she tried to talk to me, I was afraid to answer her as well.

I couldn't imagine what our *real* mother was going to do with this information. I wished she would leave other people out of this.

I carefully thought through everything I told her. I had to give the right answers, but sometimes I didn't know what "right" meant. There were so many secrets, I was afraid I'd let one slip. My *real* mother didn't know that I didn't tell anyone about her. I wondered if she was trying to trick me because she wanted *everyone* to know about her. I worried that the information I told her would give her the right to take me back. I agonized trying to figure out what Mom and Dad would want me to say. I kept my answers as brief as possible, paranoid about her writing everything down. Indeed, I wondered why my *real* mother kept taking notes.

"So, do you think you want to come and live with me?" she asked sweetly, during almost every visit.

I trembled, thinking *no way*, yet wouldn't answer her.

The moment I dreaded always came. As if the interviewing wasn't enough, it was time to smile for the camera. I was never one for insincere smiles. Sometimes my *real* mother started the photo session by scaring the living daylights out of me. She shared pictures of me as a baby with specific dates written on the back of each print. Imagine, I didn't even know she existed and she had pictures of me I'd never seen. Sometimes it was just me, sometimes me and her. Sometimes there were pictures of Andre too. Like eating the roast beef meal, it followed a pattern. We would go outside and take a picture. I moved my head this way and that. I grabbed my skirt and curtsied.

If someone else took a picture of my *real* mother, *real* sister and me, Bernyce would always be in the middle. "I'm your mother," she would announce. She wanted to see my Bucky Beaver impression in every print. *Didn't she know I hated that look?*

Questions, questions, questions. With all the questions, she never asked me how I felt or what I knew about being in a foster home. She didn't ask me what I wanted to know, for that matter. She asked about everything and everyone else around me. If she was my *real* mother, shouldn't she know that already? Honestly, I couldn't wait for the get-togethers to be over.

Getting through the final moments were the worst. My *real* mother whispered in my ear, "I love you." She tried to hug me and I leaned her way, not having any energy or desire to squeeze back. Sometimes she held my face in her hands and tried to kiss me on the lips. I moved my head to the side to avoid her. She would say, "You never know; you may want to come back." Shivers ran up and down my spine. Once again my head and heart sent the same defiant messages. *Get away from me!* screamed my head. *I just can't handle this!* cried my heart.

Sometimes I visited with Aunt Evelyn. I learned that my *real* mother wasn't allowed at some meetings so she would hide and take pictures from afar.

I still remember the meeting at the Gold Coin restaurant as Aunt Evelyn started to tell me cruel things about my foster dad.

She told me he was mean and arrogant. She said he was standing in the way of a relationship with my *real* mother. I shook my head violently. "Dad is wonderful. He is very good to me. He and Mom love me!" How I just wanted to run. How dare she! I didn't appreciate her talking about him. She was making up a story. I think she wanted me to hate him!

When the get-togethers ended, I didn't want to discuss what went on when I got back home. I couldn't talk to Mom about my *real* mother. I was still denying her existence. Plus I didn't want to hurt Mom's feelings or make Dad uneasy. I didn't want to tell Dad that someone was saying mean things about him. I knew they wanted to take away my pain and confusion. Prior to the secret being told, I trusted them so much. And I missed that.

In the past, I could always talk to Dad, but silence started to build. He peered inside my bedroom door each evening and walked cautiously toward my bed. I laid so still, looking up at my canopy trying to recapture the closeness we had shared. He sat on the edge near my pillow and I rested my head on his lap. I looked into his eyes as he stroked my hair. He didn't have to say anything. He knew I still cared for him and I knew he still loved me. I wanted to hug him. But I hugged Queenie instead.

The walls were going up. No one in my world knew about this *real* relationship and the agony it was causing. I was learning about a world belonging to many others, a world I didn't belong to. I needed to start asking questions and doing interviews myself.

My Real Sister

I was placed with the Schreiber family on the north side of Chicago when I was eight months old. I learned I had a foster mom, Jackie, and foster dad, Alex. An adopted brother, Jeff, joined our family when I was seven. Alex and Jackie's biological daughters, Pamela and Joy, were born when I was fourteen and fifteen years old. I was the only child for many years and then was the oldest child, a big sister. We lived in a nice ranch home and neighborhood, and I was treated as family. I had no reason to feel like I wasn't part of it until the secret unveiled. Unlike in Andre's life, Mom and Dad didn't tell me about being a foster child or having foster parents until they had to do so. They had decided not to use my birth name of Jackie Lynn Paul and called me Lynn Schreiber.

The social worker and Mom and Dad told me Andre (who I learned to call Andi) was placed with the Berman family on the south side of Chicago when she was two years old. I did not understand how Andi could be older than me and I not know about her. I wondered, but didn't ask, why we were separated and placed in different homes.

Her foster family included her mom, dad, an older sister and brother, who was born after Andi arrived in their home. Andi was the youngest child when she entered the home, then the middle child and big sister. They lived in a nice home and neighborhood, treating Andi as their own, yet telling her the facts of life as a foster child as soon as she could absorb and hope to understand. She used her entire birth name, Andre Joy Paul, most times. Occasionally, she used her foster family's last name, Berman.

Real mothers, *real* fathers, *real* sisters, *real* names, foster family. *What was real? What was foster?* My mind exploded with stories of each person's role in my life and how they intertwined. I couldn't find any sense to it. I was confused and wondered if Andi was, too.

She seemed to know more about me than I knew about her. When Mom and Dad spoke of Andi's and my *real* mother and father being *ours*, the word *our* sounded weird. That is when I realized what *real* meant. If they were *ours*, then we must be sisters. I feared the next *real* secret.

Mom and Dad told me Andi was a year and a half older than me. They said that since I was a baby when our *real* mother got sick, the social worker felt I needed more attention from a family that didn't have other children. After Mom and Dad adopted Jeff, I became the big sister of the family. I wondered if Andi realized we were both big sisters to little brothers in our foster families.

The fact that I had an older *real* sister just continued the stupor of the unveiling secret. I made up every excuse in the book not to get to know Andi. She lived on the south side; I lived on the north side. She had curly hair; I had straight hair. She wore jeans; I wore dresses. She knew all about me; I knew nothing about her. It didn't seem like we could be friends, let alone sisters. And, I was told not to tell anyone about her. Mom and Dad said we needed to keep the secret. I didn't know why, but I knew I had to obey; they were my parents. *Or were they my parents?*

Between being eight years old and high school, I saw Andi on occasion. It was just that, an occasion.

Andi and I joined our *real* mother and relatives at family gatherings, like a cousin's wedding or dinner party. But it was hard to understand where we belonged in that family. We were introduced as Andre and Jackie. As sisters, we met *real* aunts, uncles and cousins who hugged us with delight even though they were strangers to us - strangers who knew all about Andi and me. Yet we didn't even know each other, let alone all these other people. So, Andi and I hid away in a bathroom to escape the uncomfortable environment and our *real* mother would come looking for us. When someone called me "Jackie," it took me several moments to respond because it didn't hit me that they were speaking to me. When they called for Andre, she answered a little quicker, but once in a while, our eyes would meet as if to say, "Don't they know our names are Andi and Lynn?"

At The Visits, Andi and I shared an unspoken understanding of the notepad and camera. As Andi answered questions, she looked at me. While we learned about each other, we sometimes rolled our eyes, agreeing that taking notes was going too far. And we both dreaded picture time. Andi and I rarely stood side-by-side; our *real* mother got right between us whenever she got the chance. Or she took a picture with each of us. Once in a while she'd take a picture of just Andi and me.

One year, Mom, Dad, Jeff and I ventured to the south side of town to join my extended foster family for the holidays. I never really considered Grandma Shirley, Grandpa Nate and all the aunts, uncles and cousins of my foster mother and father as "foster." To me, they were simply Grandma, Grandpa, aunts, uncles and cousins. They were in a world not connected to my *real* mother Bernyce and sister Andi. The one thing that they had in common with Andi, though, was that they lived on the same side of town.

We always dressed our best when the whole family walked together to Temple for the high holidays on that south side of Chicago. I skipped down the sidewalk with my cousin Audrey keeping an eagle eye out for Andi along the way. I wanted to see her, but I worried if she would be welcomed to join a family not her own. *Did we belong together?*

Our big family sat in our own section at the Temple and I thought, "There's plenty of room for Andi." I wondered why she didn't join us. I wondered if our *real* mother went to Temple.

Back at Grandma's house, the adults chatted before and after meals while my cousins Audrey, Jeri and I went outside and played at the grand park right next door.

Andi usually arrived after mealtime. I peered at her standing on the sidewalk with a gentle smile on her face. I timidly walked up to her with my hands by my side, offering a welcome "Hello." She walked back to meet my cousins with me. They said hello to her, also welcoming her sincerely, and we continued to play as if she was just a neighborhood kid who came along for playtime.

I was quite the singer and the dancer ordering, "You stand here, you there, everyone turn around, clap three times and bow," to the song *Love Potion Number 9*. Andi stood and watched. I don't know why I never asked her to join us. I didn't even know if she liked to dance.

Though my *real* sister was present with the family I embraced as mine, she wasn't *embraced* as a part of that family. I wanted to understand but I was afraid to ask why we were unacknowledged sisters. *Why was she excluded from something like the holidays, which were all about family? Why could she join us in our playtime outside but was not invited to the warmth of our inside family celebration?* I never asked and no one ever explained. It just didn't seem right.

I went to Andi's foster home on occasion and Andi spent one night at my home after one of our *real* cousin's wedding.

Truthfully, I only gave Andi the time of day when I had to. My foster family never talked about her and never asked about her after my visits. All along I thought, "She's not my sister" as I drifted with the flow of constantly staged conversations, interviews and photographs. Our *real* mother boasted about her role as our mother, yet insisted, "If you're not going to get to know me, you can't know each other."

After all, as we grew older, the differences seemed more than obvious. I usually showed up like a princess with ritzy clothes, matching accessories, wiglets or falls spilling from my head, makeup to complete the presentation and a goody-two-shoes personality that would nauseate anyone. Andi, on the other hand, just showed up with her curly head of hair, old jeans, no makeup, and basically said anything that came to mind.

We had different styles; we lived in separate homes on opposite sides of town; we had different looks. I questioned why we were so opposite, yet we got along so well when we were together. I was ready to share our differences and learn the similarities.

Sibling Connection

The opportunity for creating sisterhood came when I was a junior at Niles North High School and Andi was a freshman at Northern Illinois University. She invited me to visit for a weekend. Always looking for an opportunity to have an adventure, I accepted. At first my decision to go wasn't about seeing Andi, but having an independent weekend away from home. The thought of spending so much time alone with Andi was both exciting and nerve-wracking.

I recalled The Visit at the Jewish Children's Bureau when I screamed, "She's not my sister!" I wondered what she truly thought about my outburst. Now I was going to spend time with her.

We had seldom spent big chunks of time together. And when we did, there was always an adult with us. This was the first time I'd stay with her, alone for a whole weekend, with no foster parents, *real* mother or social workers. *Could we get along? What we would talk about?* Until this time, I had kept the secret as Mom and Dad requested. But, now, I had to tell someone. I needed to talk to someone about this grand adventure with my *real* sister!

I stood in the doorway of my girlfriend Audree's kitchen as she and another friend, Ellen, sat at the dining table. I backed up against the door frame with my legs spread shoulder width to ensure a firm stance. My knees wobbled and my hands went from pushing against each side of the frame to holding my sweaty palms together tightly. Because I was shaking and teary-eyed, they looked at me with concern. If they shooed me away after learning about my secret, I was ready to run.

I had called ahead to say I had something important to tell my close friends. Audree was my best friend at high school. We were in the same hall D and, with both of our last names starting with S-C-H, we were around each other all the time. We were both in the Moriah chapter of BBG, B'nai Brith Girls, an organization for Jewish youth, and the song *Moriah* was never the same once we sang our rendition. "A way out there they had a name for wind and rain and fire...Moriah..." Standing in Audree's kitchen, I knew I was about to weather a storm. I had to tell her about my *real* sister. Because she also had a sister at Northern Illinois University, she would know about older sisters. Maybe she would even go with me to spend time with Andi.

I played with my ponytail as I fumbled with the words. I could barely look directly into Audree's or Ellen's eyes. "You know my parents," I stammered. "Well, they really aren't my parents."

My friends' eyes grew big. They leaned closer to me from their kitchen chairs and rested their chins on their palms, bracing their elbows on their knees. Their calmness was welcome and their silence allowed me to continue boldly. I quivered. I was scared of their response and the possibility they didn't want to be friends with me anymore, so I chose my words carefully. Sometimes I sped up my words to get them all out and other times I paused to collect my thoughts.

"So, your parents aren't your parents?" asked Audree. "Jeff, Pamela and Joy aren't your *real* brother and sisters?" asked Ellen. I shook my head no.

They listened to the details with a respectful nod here and there, then shared my tears as the pressure of holding it all in escaped through my sobs and shaking body. Awestruck, they had me recount the story over and over. I held my breath nervously, anticipating their feedback. Audree got up from her seat, walked over, hugged me and said, "I can't imagine how you turned out so well." She followed with, "I wondered why you didn't look like your parents." We all had a welcomed laugh. I sighed with relief. They still accepted me as their friend.

Audree's friendship proved overwhelming as her hugs embraced me and her unconditional acknowledgment gave me chills. I wasn't losing a friend; I was gaining a confidante who didn't judge me. She still thought I was wonderful. Then she offered to go to Northern Illinois University with me, saying she could visit her sister but would be nearby if I needed her. Unconditional love. It was a great feeling. I had told a secret. *My* secret.

Then I told them not to tell anyone else. "Why can't anyone know? It doesn't change anything," said Audree.

"My parents don't want anyone to know and I'm not sure why," I said, "but, I don't want anyone to look at me, or them, differently either."

My reception at home was unexpected. "I told you not to tell," shrieked Mom. I could see the hurt in her and Dad's faces. It was the first time I spoke up about the truth to others, and we were all in shock.

"Are they going to tell other people?" Mom asked. "No, but why does it matter? My friends are still my friends," I stuttered as the tears starting flowing. "Audree and Ellen won't think of us any differently!" I shouted. Mom and Dad were angry. The secret was out. But they still wouldn't tell me why they didn't want anyone to know.

The next weekend, Audree pulled up to the house and I carried my night bag to her car. Mom and Dad stood at the door, motionless. I walked back to them, staring into their sad eyes. I don't know if they were afraid I wouldn't come back or if our relationship would change even more. I wanted to ask questions, but the words wouldn't come out of my mouth. Mom and Dad offered no information, only silence. I just gave each of them a hug and said, "I have to do this. Everything will be okay." I wished they both agreed.

During the one-and-a-half-hour ride to the university, Audree and I chatted nervously. We talked about Audree's relationship with her older sister, but I didn't have much to say about Andi because we hadn't learned much about each other. We didn't have childhood memories together to share. I didn't even know what she was studying in college.

In fact, I became concerned about how Andi would treat me since I had snubbed her for so long. She almost always initiated any interaction and I'd respond minimally. I was nervous and excited all at once. Luckily, my fears vanished the moment I stepped out of the car. Without hesitation, Andi greeted me with a big hug and said, "Do you mind if I introduce you as my little sister?"

I couldn't believe what I just heard. I glanced back at Audree still sitting in the car and wearing a huge smile. She returned a big nod of YES! Closing my eyes as if it was all a dream, I repeated to myself, *Can she introduce me as her little sister?* I opened them to see Andi standing before me with her arms outstretched. We hugged for what seemed like an eternity. I stood back and whispered to her, "Thank you."

She wanted me to be her little sister despite the distance of our relationship. I smiled widely. I felt like a celebrity as she introduced me to her friends and they responded by saying, "We've heard so much about you." I couldn't imagine what they had heard. All I knew was *I was with my big sister.* I belonged. I loved her to pieces. I introduced her to Audree. "This is my sister, Andi," I said with pride. Audree got out of the car and gave both of us a hug. She gave me a reassuring smile and whispered, "Have fun. I'm only a phone call away."

Andi had never had the opportunity of introducing a little sister because she was the little sister in her foster family. I had never had anyone introduce me as a little sister because I was the big sister in my family. Now we had our *real* places in life, as sisters. *Real* was becoming more defined.

Andi was so free spirited, a "wild coed" by definition. I wanted connection so badly, so I just took it all in. I noticed her boyfriend's name spelled out on her stomach. She explained she put masking tape on and then got a suntan, so she had a "tattoo" of her love. She told jokes and we laughed. While she laughed openly, I remained guarded.

We walked swiftly across the campus in the morning rain chatting about our lives. She was worried her wild hair would frizz the longer we stayed in the rain, so she motioned for me to stay on the sidewalk to wait for cars to pass but she ran across the street through the traffic.

I watched as a car came speeding up the road toward us, then heard the screech of the tires. As I stood on the curb, I watched as Andi's body flew up on the front hood of the car, rolled onto the windshield, back down the hood and fell to the ground, motionless. My heart was instantly torn apart. "That is my sister lying on the ground!" I screamed. My instinctual love for her rose to the front of my mind. I ran over and put my face close to hers, sprawling over her like a mother bear protecting her cubs. People gathered as the driver of the car raced around to us on the ground. Andi looked up at me and smiled. At that moment, I rejoiced inside, exuberant that she was alive. Her smile melted my heart. She wanted me to care. I did. Instantly, I cared. It was a magical and memorable time for us amid this chaos.

Someone called 9-1-1 and the sirens blared. Andi waved to me from the stretcher as she was lifted inside the ambulance. While the driver of the car that hit her stood by in anguish, we began to relax knowing Andi would be fine. A student drove me to the hospital.

The diagnosis from the doctors at the emergency room reported nothing more than bruises, but Andi and I knew the greater prognosis was the deepened connection of our souls. And Andi had a new story to tell. "I ran in front of the car on purpose to make it a weekend we would both never forget and bring us closer together," she told her friends.

We did grow closer together. The accident made time for us to get to know each other. She needed to rest so most of our visit took place with her lying, and my sitting on her dorm room bed. We needed to heal the loss of our childhood together.

That weekend, we talked and talked. We found out things that were different and the same between us. We spoke about our families, our schools and our friends. She spoke of her travels and I spoke of my new car given to me by my parents on my sixteenth birthday. She told of her foster family and how she knew everything about me and my family on the north side. I spoke about my foster family and about how I knew nothing about her and her family on the south side.

For the first time, I felt I could celebrate our differences. We laughed when she just blurted out a thought, but I hesitated and chose my words before I spoke. "Just say it," she would chide me. We made fun of each other's preferences for clothing styles. She favored worn-out jeans and T-shirts and I liked coordinated outfits. "Do you have bows to match?" she chuckled. We learned that for all her friends who knew about me, only a couple of my friends were aware of her. I suddenly felt sad and embarrassed that no one knew about this spectacular person who was my big sister.

During the weekend, we decided to phone our *real* mother, whom together we referred to as "Colorado." She lived in Colorado so we agreed that we were both comfortable referring to her that way. Andi had kept in touch with her outside our scheduled get-togethers and occasions. I, on the other hand, only saw her when I had to as mandated by the system. But that weekend, we wanted her to know that her daughters were spending time together and that we spoke about her, too. We didn't know how she would respond. We were concerned she might feel jealous that she wasn't with us, but hoped she would be happy for our new sisterhood connection.

As Andi dialed the phone, I realized I had just accepted Andi as my sister. However, I still didn't accept Colorado as my *real* mother, our *real* mother.

Andi spoke to Colorado first, excitedly telling her about my visit. She told her about introducing me as her little sister and the car accident. We were on Andi's bed and I shrugged my shoulders in disbelief that my *real* mother, *real* sister and I were communicating about our lives. As I jotted notes on a small pad while she held the phone, we tried to come up with something personal to tell Colorado. Andi blurted out, "Lynn, I mean Jackie, just got her period." I was mortified. In one instant, I went from Lynn to Jackie. In the second instant, I got embarrassed. I had never shared anything so personal with Colorado or anyone for that matter. I blushed brightly and headed toward the door.

Andi started to laugh wildly and I turned around glaring at her. She playfully dropped the phone and continued laughing uncontrollably. I was so bewildered. I jumped back on the bed, then started laughing with her. *What was so funny?* I didn't care. I was laughing with my sister and it felt good.

Then she picked up the phone, muffled the mouthpiece and whispered, "Mothers want to know when their daughters start their periods." We laughed together. I was aware that this was a rare connection between my *real* sister and me and now our *real* mother.

I had never before thought of Andi or Colorado as family. Now, a mother and her two daughters were laughing about my period. Wow! Colorado was my *real* mother. That strong realization laid its roots in me like never before.

In three days, we built our foundation of friendship and sisterhood. Andi and I found out that, although we were different in so many ways, we had so much in common. It was fun to be a part of each other's worlds of unconditional love, so we made a pact to stay connected through phone calls and letters. We agreed to see each other whenever we could arrange a visit alone. Andi taught me that I didn't have to keep secrets anymore. I was proud to call her my big sister. I wanted everyone to know her.

Not only did I enjoy being the little sister; I was thrilled to learn about my big sister. I belonged to someone. I didn't feel lonely anymore.

I hugged her and thanked her for not giving up on me. We stood together for a long time. When Audree pulled up in her car, I gave Andi one last hug and got in. As we drove away, I glanced back with tears in my eyes. We looked at each other, sharing an unspoken understanding of our new *real* relationship.

Colorado

Andi maintained a relationship with our mother by phone, and visited her. But even after that call from Andi's dorm room, I still kept the connection with her at a distance.

After all, my foster parents still fulfilled the parental role in my life. I continued to refer to them as Mom and Dad especially when I hit certain milestones. They stood by my side celebrating my Bat Mitzvah, which marked my entry into adulthood. They threw a lavish sixteenth birthday party for me at a local event center, buying me a special outfit and arranging to have my hair done at the beauty shop. My high school graduation dress was stunning and the swimming party that followed was a huge hit. For my gift, Mom and Dad supported me by convincing the foster care authorities to allow me to go on a seven-week trip to Israel, organized by a local youth group. After the adventure I was headed off to college.

I set my sights on attending a top ten university; University of Illinois. My friend Darlene was already accepted and I adamantly wanted to join her. I applied under the School of Business and the rejection letter brought me to my knees. Determined to attend, my family drove to Champaign and I interviewed with the College of Agriculture. I would do whatever it took to be with my friend at U of I. I was accepted. Colorado and Andi weren't at any of these celebrations or a part of any of the decisions, which seemed appropriate. My life with them, while becoming acceptable and understandable, was separate from my life with Mom and Dad.

I started to think about the role of our mother in my life with more respect as I entered college. I started to call her more often. Maybe I found it easier to phone her because I was away from Mom and Dad. I always wanted to protect Mom and Dad from direct conversations with or about my mother because I didn't want to minimize their role as my parents. But now I was ready to get to know Colorado and call her my mother.

I felt the time came when I wanted to talk to my mother about my relationship with Andi, especially because she knew we spent sister time together that weekend at Northern Illinois University. I tiptoed around that topic because I detected jealousy from her swift responses and ability to change the conversation. I knew that this was the start of my acceptance of our entire *real* family.

Indeed, I couldn't imagine how this mother felt having her children taken from her.

Andi and I believed that she didn't necessarily want us to have our own relationship if she couldn't have one with us as well. She'd still sit between us and disrupt the flow of our conversations. She loved us desperately, though. Her eyes revealed a loneliness and a longing for a loving mother-daughter relationship.

"You know, I could have taken you back," she said from time to time. I avoided eye contact or any kind of response. I wished that she had the patience and confidence to believe that we could have a relationship. After all, Andi and I had just started celebrating our connection in the recent past. We were both successful college students. I simply wanted her to celebrate our sisterhood and our achievements. The past was not our fault.

During this time, I learned she had a case plan created by the social service system. In order to get Andi and me back, she had to fulfill many requirements including stability of an apartment and a job. But as time passed, Andi and I grew older and more bonded to our respective foster families. It became too late for her to take us back. My foster family was MY family. I never wanted one family to feel less important than the other, but it was clear *real* didn't mean *my* family. I didn't want to leave my foster family. However, my *real* mother never relinquished parental rights so Mom and Dad never had the opportunity to adopt me therefore relegating me to long term foster care.

Until I was a junior in college, Audree and Ellen were the only confidantes who knew I was a foster child. While I continued to develop a relationship with my mother, until that year I even kept the secret from my sorority sisters. I loved college and I loved my sorority. The sisters of Sigma Delta Tau really brought a new definition of "sister" to me. Darlene was the president while I was the vice president. I was consumed in our new family of sisters also serving as pledge trainer and Panhellenic representative. Many of my sisters and I were big sisters and pledge mothers not only within our sorority but to the boys of Zeta Beta Tau, Pikes and Sigma Nu. I worked at the radio station and a local magazine. I was a waitress and a bartender. I danced the weekend at the MDA danceathon. Indeed, college represented the best years of my life.

That junior year, my mother had triple by-pass surgery and I felt it was a time to care openly. Instead of going on the

Florida spring vacation I'd planned with my sorority sisters, I decided to visit her in Colorado.

Just as I had done with Audree and Ellen sitting at the kitchen table back home, I gathered several of my sorority sisters into one of the back bedrooms in the house. My closest friend, Darlene, joined several others to learn about my change of plans.

"What is this all about?" they whispered to each other as they entered the room and sat on the two beds on the far wall. I boldly unfolded my secret. I didn't want my sorority sisters to feel sorry for me or think differently about me. They listened intensely as I shared the details of my journey in foster care. Their respectful silence, only interrupted by sniffles and then grins, washed over me in a feeling of acceptance.

They knew I wasn't going to Florida. And they embraced me when they learned why I was going to Colorado. Several wrote me letters wishing me strength and expressing their admiration. They wanted to learn about my mother and sister. After all, they were my sisters, too.

My mother was thrilled with my visit. She had made it through the surgery and was well on her way to a full recovery. We spent many hours sitting in her family room just saying nothing. Being together at such an important time said so much. Her surgery was all about the will to live and we began to live with a stronger mother-daughter connection.

Several years earlier she had married Bill, her high school prom date. Bill welcomed me with open arms to their home. I don't know what he knew about Andi and me, but nothing interfered with our quest to get to know each other.

During the visit, my mother asked Bill to bring out a picture box. With each picture, she shared a memory of different relatives and friends. Seeing pictures of Andi and me, I strongly felt the loss of our relationship as the dates rolled through the picture books. In them was an obvious absence of pictures of Andi and me, particularly at family get-togethers. I saw pictures of only Andi. I saw pictures of only me. We talked openly and honestly about the time we missed. She spoke through tears about her heartbreak of missing out on motherhood. "Let's be happy for what we have now," I whispered to her as we hugged good-bye.

After my trip to Colorado, Andi and I spoke about the experience and the trips she'd made to our mother as well. Sharing our separate connections with her brought Andi and I closer together. Having lost out on so much time with each other and our mother, we worked hard to create a relationship. Just as blood held us together, all of our souls started to connect.

We started to belong.

What's My Name?

As a youth in care, my college education was paid for by the state. That meant that I'd have to use my legal birth name. So I had to strategically time my registration because I knew I would be standing in the P line for Paul rather than the S line for Schreiber. I didn't want my college friends to think I didn't know my own name.

I remember the first day of second grade. Miss Kurzweg was taking attendance. I suddenly heard her say, "Jackie Lynn Paul." I froze in my seat and didn't say a word. "Jackie Paul?" I continued to sit like a statue. When she called the name for the third time, I slowly walked up to her desk and said quietly, "I want to be called Lynn Schreiber."

I learned that I was registered in the school by my birth name, not my foster given name. The registrar hadn't updated my foster family's preference.

Approaching my 23rd birthday, I was officially on my own. I had emancipated from the system and The University of Illinois paved the way to my degree in communications. Now it was my turn to use my voice. A career in communications lie ahead. Though having my own family was a distant thought, having my own name was a must.

Both my birth name Jackie Lynn Paul and foster family name Lynn Schreiber followed me with purpose and logic, secrecy and caution, bitterness and pride over my life span. My foster family changed my original name to Lynn Schreiber in our daily lives. On one hand, the reason for the first name change was religious. On the other hand, it was convenient and unassuming to have the same last name as my foster family and avoid questions why my name was different. I don't know if the social worker would have had to approve a name change earlier, but I knew it was my decision now. At eight years old when I found out I was a foster child, I wasn't going to be called by my *real* name. At 23, I wanted my *real* and legal name to be Lynn Schreiber.

While using Jackie Lynn Paul was favored by my biological family, Lynn Schreiber was the choice of my foster family. My case files indicate I had problems with the different names. Honestly, I didn't know I had a choice. Even though I was one person, I knew that with one family I was Jackie Lynn Paul and with the other I was Lynn Schreiber. I had to remind myself to answer to the name of the environment and the people in it, and I don't remember feeling mad or confused. I just remember acquiescing to those around me with respect and showmanship.

Mother could still call me Jackie as she always did. I know she felt bitter about the change and never called me Lynn.

On this January in 1978 I was proud to be Lynn Schreiber.

Finally, it was my decision to officially change my name. My life, as I knew it, was Lynn Schreiber. Almost everyone knew me, as I knew myself, as Lynn. I didn't have a middle name, but that never bothered me. I had never asked, or even wondered why.

I wanted to officially be known as Lynn, Lynn Schreiber, knowing that someday when I married, the decree would only be legal with my legal name. A marriage to Lynn Schreiber when I was legally Jackie Lynn Paul wouldn't be *real*.

So I filed a Decree For Change of Name with the Circuit Court of Cook County, Illinois. The document screamed, "County Department, Chancery Divorce Division" from the top of the page. I guessed I was divorcing my name.

The *Chicago Daily Law Bulletin*, a newspaper of general circulation published in Cook County, Illinois, ran the few-sentence petition for several consecutive weeks prior to January 23, 1978. If anyone challenged my desire to change my name, they were to step forward. Quite honestly, I didn't tell my mother or Andi about the decree. Nobody needed to be hurt and I didn't need to be questioned.

Mom, Dad and I didn't discuss my reason to officially change my name. I simply announced my plan and assumed they would be happy and proud. They silently hugged me and Dad willingly drove me to the Cook County courthouse.

I took a seat on one of the many dark wood benches facing the judge's stand. The foreman asked everyone to rise as the judge took his seat behind the big cherry expanse at the far side of the room. I slowly read the petition in my hands for the umpteenth time. There were so many legal words and phrases. I just had to assume each word meant I could legally change my name, that I was filling out the proper paperwork and attending court, as required.

The document read, "The conditions mentioned and specified in an Act of the General Assembly of the State of Illinois entitled An Act to Revise the Law in Relation to Names approved Feb. 25, 1874 and in force July 1, 1874 have been complied with…" I wasn't the first person to request a name change.

Judge Nathan S. Coleman called "Case of Jackie Lynn Paul" in a thundering voice. My dad motioned to me. I stood and we walked toward the bench side by side. On tiptoes, I peered up at Judge Coleman as he looked at the documents and then at me.

"Young lady, why do you want to change your name?" his thundering voice changed to a whisper.

"I was in foster care and I want to take the name given to me by my foster family and known to all," I quietly answered.

"Permission granted," Judge Coleman responded.

It was that quick and that easy. It was that life-changing and that difficult. I had stood up for myself and the judge respected me.

I walked over to the side desk and watched the clerk review the decree. She read, "It is therefore ordered, adjudged and decreed that the said petitioner's name be, and the same is hereby changed from Jackie Lynn Paul to Lynn Schreiber by which said last-mentioned name shall be hereafter known and called."

She signed the form.

"January 23, 1978, Margaret M. Fine, Clerk"

I was. I am. Lynn Schreiber. The *real* Lynn Schreiber. My name belonged to me.

Marriage of Families

For several years after I graduated from college, I reveled in a position as sales promotion director at Combined Insurance Company of America in Chicago. The company philosophy of PMA, Positive Mental Attitude, filled every vein in my body. Motivating 300 insurance sales people on a daily basis was a vibrant order. Led by me, we chanted "I feel happy, healthy and terrific" and rang cowbells in celebration of sales quotas met.

I often thought of the man of my dreams and envisioned a wedding filled with love and support from both my biological and foster families. I fantasized about all of the Jewish traditions: the canopy over my head, the glass-breaking under my groom's foot, the blessing over the challah bread and the toasts of celebration with wine. I envisioned the guests dancing the traditional hora and raising my new husband and me on chairs as we moved to the festive music with a handkerchief dangled between us.

Little did I expect a drama filled with bitterness, selfishness, confusion and outright target practice that we experienced at Andi's wedding and at mine several years later.

The dynamics were set at Andi's bridal shower at Kon-Tiki Ports on Michigan Avenue. It was apparent our mother was going for the power play. At the head table, instead of my sitting on one side of Andi and her on the other, she sat between us. Flashbacks of being eight years old at the restaurant entered my mind. She spoke ad nauseam of her quest to keep Andi and I together under her roof. Bitterness seeped out with jealousy that Andi and I got along and that we didn't have the same close relationship with her.

The affair was attended by some of our cousins whom I still didn't know very well. Andi's foster mother and sister were excluded. My foster mother was excluded. Aunt Evelyn planned this party with our mother in mind and she ran the guest list. Andi's friends attended, and we made small talk, yet I didn't have much to say because I didn't know them. They knew I was Andi's little sister, but until that moment, most hadn't seen us together.

My parents and I were invited to Andi's wedding to be held in the back yard of her home. She was marrying Bob, a wonderful man she'd met while serving as a counselor at a camp for children and adults with cerebral palsy. All I knew about Bob was his love for children and for my sister. That made me happy for Andi. However, I sadly realized that Andi and I had never shared thoughts about boyfriends like sisters usually do. We'd never taken the opportunity to discuss our dates or dreams for husbands.

I also knew Bob wasn't Jewish and that fact, tied to the wedding taking place before sunset on a Saturday, already had our mother off kilter.

The wedding day arrived. I took a deep breath as I stepped out of the car, holding tightly to the hand of my boyfriend, Craig. He felt my trepidation as I leaned against him and met my eyes to give an unspoken gift of understanding. I was going to a place I hadn't been before.

Our mother and Bill were present. Mom and Dad were with me. Andi's foster parents were around. Guests who were part of Andi's life were there, but even though I was the bride's sister, I didn't know most of them. Andi and I just didn't have the opportunity to spend quality time with each other's friends or respective extended foster families.

Some of our relatives attended, but I didn't know how to receive or act toward them. I was nervous at the prospect of mixing the families, wondering who knew what or who was thinking about whom. Mostly I was trying to find clarity in each person's role in the wedding.

At one point, our mother was rambling on in the living room of Andi's home. I stood stiffly in the doorway poised to escape at any moment. Craig was at my side as Mom and Dad stood nearby. My heart raced. My mother and my mom were in the same space. At this festive occasion, I didn't know how to be festive. Andi's foster mother and father were in the space too. Our mother continued to babble on, front and center, about Andi and Bob's marriage. An unnerving aura enveloped the room.

Craig put his arm around my shoulders and pulled me closer. He tried to shield me from the discomfort of the scene, but I felt anything but comfortable.

I couldn't wait to get out of there. I looked for the minister to head toward the canopy outdoors. I wanted the ceremony to start and end. My eyes darted from Andi and Bob, to Mom and Dad, to the canopy and to the clock. Inside, I wanted to celebrate my sister's marriage with wide smiles and hugs. Outside, I could barely muster a grin, so I stood apart from the guests of honor. It shouldn't have mattered who was related to whom, yet I couldn't help but focus on the confusion of belonging. I wanted to believe that the *real* and foster families all belonged to each other.

I walked through Andi's back yard being cordial. I felt badly that I didn't know much about her foster family. Mostly, I was proud Andi was following her heart, her way. As it came time to walk down the aisle as her bridesmaid, I looked to Craig for confidence. Mom and Dad sat by him with stiff bodies and stern looks, their discomfort with the mingling families obvious. I caught them out of the corner of my eye. They had come to this event for me, and that's all that mattered.

I was a lost soul, being embraced by my sister as her sister, which was an incredible honor, yet I was choking inside. Andi was including me, yet somehow my soul felt excluded.

Once the glass broke underfoot, I bolted out of there. While I truly wanted to feel a part of the joy of the occasion, tension overruled and I couldn't let my guard down. I didn't know where I belonged.

Daddy's Little Girl Says Good-Bye

Before long, Craig and I went our separate ways. Because I wanted total independence away from home and my past love, I moved to Atlanta where I found a position at ESPN after working for another insurance company. I had studied communications and was "living it" for a new sports programming network. After successfully opening the company's southwest office, I got transferred to Dallas to open another regional office.

Then I got the startling call. All Mom had to say was, "Dad had a stroke." I took the next plane back to Chicago and a fast taxi to the hospital to join Mom.

I really was Daddy's little girl and I needed to be by his side. I took his hand in mine and tears ran down our cheeks. "Everything will be fine," he choked. I laid down beside him until he fell asleep. Mom stood up from the bedside chair and motioned that it was time for us to leave. I kissed Dad on the forehead and we went back to her house.

I heard the phone ring in the middle of the night and a few seconds later Mom's footsteps came to my door.

"Dad is sick. Wake the other kids and get dressed," she said in a quivering voice. Within moments, my favorite Uncle

Murphy was parked outside and we ran toward his car. The middle of the night eeriness deepened my fright. I closed my eyes praying Dad was okay.

Uncle Murphy pulled up in front of Michael Reiss Hospital. Mom, my brother, sisters and I ran through the revolving door and up the elevator to the intensive care unit. The doctor met us at the nurse's station.

"He's in a coma," we were told. I put my arms around Mom's shoulders and Jeff, Pam and Joy cuddled. We slowly walked into Dad's room and surrounded his bed. Mom and I each took a hand. We cried. The doctor came in and explained that Dad no longer had brain activity and that we needed to make a decision about life support. Uncle Murphy came into the room and tried to comfort all of us.

We decided to let Dad rest in peace. Mom and the kids said their good-byes and Uncle Murphy walked with them to the waiting room. I remained in the room at Dad's bedside holding his hand. The nurse looked at me sadly as she turned off the machine that was keeping Dad alive. I watched the heart monitor go from peaks and valleys to a solid line. "Goodbye Daddy, I will love you forever," I whispered in his ear.

My Wedding

Not too long after Dad's death, I met Chuck Price at a cable television event. He worked for Nickelodeon. He was blowing up balloons and sharing them with children who came by his exhibit in the mall. I watched from my booth down the aisle as each boy and girl eagerly received a gift with delight. I was enamored with how Chuck interacted with the children, as if he was a child himself. That evening we went two-stepping after a dinner event with the other exhibitors.

In November, 1982, I decided to resign from my position with Group W Satellite Communications who had courted me from ESPN earlier that year. It had been five months since Chuck moved from Dallas to Denver and distance between us was tearing me apart. I needed to find out if he was "the one."

I knew my decision to move to Denver was right when one of the finest mentors of my life, GWSC's Vice President Roy Mehlman, called and asked, "Who is this guy you are moving for?"

"I have to find out if he's the one, Roy," I responded.

Roy wouldn't accept my resignation and insisted I work out of my new home in Denver.

Since Dad's passing, Mom and I spoke every couple of weeks. While she missed me, she was thrilled I had a good job. We talked about Pam, Joy and Jeff, and her card games with her girlfriends. She loved to play cards and it helped her deal with losing Dad.

I stood in the kitchen of my Dallas apartment, took a deep breath and dialed Mom's phone number. I paced, anxiously waiting for someone to answer. "Mom, I'm moving to Denver," I said excitedly the moment she said hello. "I've been promoted at Group W."

"Congratulations, I'm proud of you."

Until now, I hadn't told Mom about Chuck because she and Dad had zero tolerance for interfaith dating. I thought that talking about my job first would minimize her reaction to my moving to be with a non-Jewish man.

"I've been seeing a guy, Chuck. He's in Denver and I need to find out if he is "the one."

"Is he Jewish?" she asked without hesitation.

"No," I answered.

Silence echoed on the other end of the phone - a silence that lasted for years. She had threatened me before with disownment if I even had a relationship outside of our faith. Now I was moving away to be with a Christian man, and the writing was on the wall. As she hung up without even saying "good-bye," "I trust your judgment," or "be well," I felt I'd been stabbed through my heart. I had spent so much of my life trying to please her and make her proud. She had just said she was proud and now I was losing that. I wanted her to be happy for me. But, it wasn't about *me*. It was about *her*. I had to let go. While my heart sank with disappointment, I turned my thoughts to moving in with Chuck. Now where did I belong?

My mother lived in Pueblo, Colorado, only 60 miles south of my new home in Denver. Since Mom had completely disowned me, the door opened for her to step in. She was all too happy to have me living down the highway, and we met on occasion at her home or during her trips to Denver.

While I worked out of our apartment in Denver, I reported weekly to an office in Los Angeles. Each Monday, I got up at 4:30 a.m. and Chuck took me to the airport. Then I would fly to L.A. and grab a taxi to arrive at the office by 8 a.m. An all-day meeting ensued until I caught the 6 p.m. flight back to Denver. Chuck was always waiting at curbside arrivals. On one particular night several months after the move, we went to our favorite restaurant for dinner. I was sharing my daily frustrations of the office staff meeting as we sat across from one another in a booth. He interrupted my chatter and asked, "Are you done yet?" It was apparent he had something to say. I immediately closed my mouth when I saw him reach into his coat pocket and take out a little box. He looked at me with hopeful eyes and asked, "I was wondering if you would be my wife?"

I couldn't sit still. I couldn't talk. The proposal came from nowhere. I started crying. I flew to the other side of the booth to sit beside him, looking from him to the ring. I realized somebody really loved me. Somebody really wanted me. He wanted me despite the disownment, despite the skeletons in my closet of a life in foster care. He loved me for me. At that very moment, I loved him back so very much.

We drove home in euphoria and I picked up the phone to call friends who lived nearby. They arrived at our apartment to celebrate with a bottle of champagne. Then I called Lane, Audree, Darlene, Barb and Shelley. My friends in Chicago, no matter the distance, were thrilled at my happiness.

I called Mom, but she wouldn't come to the phone even though Pam begged her to. I was heartbroken. Then I called my mother. She was upset Chuck wasn't Jewish, but offered congratulations. She asked questions about wedding plans I hadn't even thought about yet. Then I called Andi. She was so happy for me.

Chuck and I planned our own wedding. High on Lookout Mountain overlooking Denver, we chose this particular site for its beauty and nature. We knew our out-of-town guests would enjoy the experience of the Rocky Mountains.

Chuck agreed we could get married by a rabbi. How ironic that while one mother disowned me and another was displeased with my new union, I still longed for a Jewish ceremony. We searched the state and visited with local rabbis, ministers and religious studies professors. We were open to having both a rabbi and minister officiate. All steps pointed to only two rabbis who would consider conducting an interfaith marriage in Denver.

Chuck and I had lunch with one of the rabbis and spoke of our mutual agreement to have a rabbi officiate. However, we couldn't meet his financial requirements. So we met with another rabbi who said he wouldn't do it, but we could pay for his colleague to fly in from Los Angeles. In the end, the challenge to have a rabbi officiate our wedding ceremony didn't set well, so we opted for a judge, wrote our own vows, and planned for the canopy and the breaking of the glass.

Mom didn't even acknowledge the wedding invitation, but after one and a half years of no contact, I anticipated a "no show" from her, as well as from Pam and Joy. They shared the same feelings about interfaith marriage but Jeff planned to attend the wedding.

My mother replied that she would attend with Bill. The very prospect of Mother attending the wedding caused a flutter of anxiety, as I realized most invited guests did not know my history. I was certain she would want to be introduced as my mother, and there was no doubt she would work the room and leave many people open-mouthed as they courteously tried to figure out who was *this* mother, Bernyce. Most of them only knew my mom, Jackie.

The horrible thought that my wedding would turn into a soap opera pushed me to tell my story in advance to many of my friends. I was hoping to avoid hushed talks and provide some kind of comfortable welcome for my mother. They listened attentively with few questions and respectful nods.

Many of my long-time friends planned to come to Denver for the wedding. A week before the big day, Barb, my friend since kindergarten, arrived to help with the last-minute details of the celebration. We ran around confirming wedding plans and pampering ourselves silly.

The day before the wedding, Barb followed me in her rental car as we drove out of the apartment complex where Chuck and I lived. I was on my way to a meeting and she was going to visit a friend. The FedEx man caught me at the corner and motioned me out of the car, waving an envelope. I pulled over and stepped out to the curb, signed his board and took the envelope from his hand. My heart sank as I glanced down to see Mom's name. Barb must have seen my face drop so she jumped from her car to be at my side. The shock of the moment sent me into a quick panic attack. I halted the FedEx man and tried to force the envelope back into his hands.

Then I withdrew, knowing I had to face the reality of whatever was inside. I longed for congratulations - "Honey, I'll be there for you. Sorry for missing out on the happiness of your life." But I also knew the cold truth that I wouldn't find anything close to good wishes.

I opened the FedEx package and took out a plain white number-10 envelope. It shook in my hand. LYNN, in capital letters with a simple blue line running underneath, was outlined in black ink on the front.

Standing there in the street, I opened the envelope and read the letter out loud. Tears streamed down my face onto the paper. "Lynn, you know how much your father loved you. You think he would accept your marriage. As you know, he never did anything on the spur of the moment. I am sending you the portion of his will that has to do with you."

I trembled as I unfolded the other document. At the top it read, "Second codicil to the will of Alex Schreiber" and "DRAFT" was stamped across the top. I noticed a black marker through six sentences and something torn off on the bottom of the sheet of paper. My eyes reached the Fourth Article, 2, where I saw my name…my names.

"I give the sum of (this area is blacked out with an ink marker) to our mutually acknowledged child, Lynn Schreiber (also sometimes known as Jackie Lynn Paul), if she survives me and if she be either unmarried or married to a man of the Jewish faith who was born of parents who were both also born of (not converted to) the Jewish faith. If neither of the preceding conditions are met, I give her the sum of ONE DOL-LAR ($1.00)."

This was an official decree of disownment. I was labeled *a mutually acknowledged child*. I realized I was slotted into yet another category. I was not their daughter, but their foster daughter. It showed that if I did abide by the rules of the document, he would will to me $5,000.

Thank goodness for Barb who took the envelope from my hand and reassured me that this devious act was not of my doing. I didn't deserve it. As I stood there with hunched shoulders, she cried with me. Perhaps I should have been relieved that a final decision was made. But I felt empty, betrayed and deeply hurt. I ached with intensity so strong, so overwhelming, and so uncontrollable. I wanted to belong again.

Uncle Murphy walked me down the aisle that lovely August day. Those who meant the most to me traveled from near and far to share my wedding celebration. Darlene was my maid of honor. Andi was delighted to be a bridesmaid and never questioned my choice of having Darlene closest to me. My cousin Jeri stood with Darlene and Andi. Lane sat in the front row with my friend Amy who flew in from Boston. Amy and I had forged a deep friendship after sharing the journey to Israel. My mother sat on the inside end of the aisle with Bill next to her.

The judge had Chuck and I face the guests as the ceremony unfolded. I stood directly in Mother's view and could see sadness written all over her face. I didn't know why. While Andi shared our celebration with happiness, I had hoped that our mother would feel the same way. I wanted sheer unification of her and her daughters together. As I stood in the receiving line, she and Bill followed in line with the guests. She stepped toward me and I whispered, "Please just be happy for me and the fact that we are all together." She was silent and only offered a hug. After the receiving line broke up, I looked for her.

"Andi, do you know where Colorado is?" I asked, tilting my head in curiosity.

"She left," answered Andi giving me a hug, but not offering any explanation.

I learned later that our mother was bitter at her lack of participation in the wedding. She didn't walk down the aisle, nor did she receive a corsage. Forgetting the flowers and her part in the ceremony was my oversight. It just didn't even enter my mind; she didn't fit that definition of a mother for me.

I took my place as Chuck Price's bride. We belonged together. He was "the one."

Passages

Three years after I hung up with Mom on the day of disownment, my grandmother called.

"Lynnie, your mom is very sick. She had a stroke. She has some loss of movement on the right side of her face and body. She's in the hospital and wants to see you and meet your husband," she said, softly weeping.

Without elaboration or hesitation, I responded, "We'll be there."

I pondered why Mom didn't make the call herself, but it didn't really matter. This bright light overshadowed her stubborn style. The invitation said enough. I always wanted to be sure I did everything I could to rekindle the relationship. Now there was a flicker of hope.

Chuck and I entered Weiss Memorial Hospital in Chicago, and walked through the very same hallways after my dad had his stroke. Chuck stood at the doorway of her room as I slowly approached her bed. Her eyes expressed words she would not allow herself to say. I knew she was sorry. Taking her hand in mine, I told her I was thankful for the call.

"I'd like you to meet my husband," I said, looking at Chuck.

He stepped next to me, putting his arm around my shoulders. "Nice to meet you," he said, looking at mom and then back at me.

She reached for his hand. "Don't take it personally that I haven't accepted you."

Mom and Chuck spoke with outward appearances of a happy new connection and acceptance. I mused, wondering how could he take anything personally when she had never given him a chance to be her son-in-law.

After that reunion, Mom and I exchanged phone calls regularly. Her right lower body didn't recover from the stroke so she used a wheelchair, receiving support from Pam and Joy who still lived with her. Sometimes she and Chuck shared a conversation during those calls. After so many years of feeling uncomfortable with the pressure of being disowned and not knowing how to find acceptance, we finally had a relationship. I felt I belonged again.

During this peaceful time, I was filled with a sense of wholeness. Mom quickly came to mind when I had exciting news to share. That's why I phoned her first to announce my pregnancy. I had hoped that since she had finally accepted my husband, she would accept my first-born baby.

"Mom, you are going to be a Grandma," I said boastfully.

"That's wonderful, honey. When? How are you?" she asked anxiously.

"Mom, there is something else I want to tell you," I said with a huge grin on my face.

"I'm listening," she said in a high pitched voice of anticipation.

"We are going to name the baby after Dad, whether it's a boy or girl."

I heard her cry through the phone lines. In this moment, I gave her and Dad the ultimate honor of pure forgiveness.

I cried, too, for I had touched her stubborn soul and found peace in making her so happy. *What better way to rebuild our lives than with the entrance of a new life.* I wanted to hold on to that moment forever.

As I progressed in my pregnancy, the morning sickness overwhelmed me. Each day through the first three months, I grew weaker from the constant vomiting. Finally, I was hospitalized. Mom shared her concern wonderfully. I hadn't anticipated such love. She phoned daily. She concerned herself with my eating. She stepped back into the role of mother and into the role of grandmother-to-be with grace and grandeur. I was thrilled to receive her love in this way.

When Addison was born, we named him for my dad, Alex. In the Jewish religion, we use the first letter of the name of the honored person's English or Hebrew name and select a name starting with the same letter.

Mom showered Addison with gifts. Our first visit brought tears of joy.

My mother was thrilled with the news, too. She filled our home with gifts.

Andi was thrilled that now we could be sisters and mothers together.

I was ecstatic that both of my mothers and my sister were happy for me, and proud to be grandmas and an aunt.

My first Mother's Day approached. Standing in the greeting card aisle, I took cards out of their slots with trembling hands. I spent hours thinking about each mother and choosing cards filled with sincerity and *reality.*

The standard sentiment *Thanks for always being there for me* always hurt the most. I wished it had been true. It was tough to find cards that honored my mothers in a way that made sense so I usually selected ones with a simple message of thanks. I chose beautiful grandmother cards from Addison as well.

Mom was ailing as summer came to a close. Her stroke had started to take its toll and diabetes had entered her world.

"How about Addison and I come to visit you for the High Holidays," I said, hoping to lift her spirits and give her something to look forward to that fall of 1987.

"That would be the best medicine. I can't wait to get my arms around Addison…and you," she said tearfully.

Mom rarely spoke such words and I felt those arms around me through the phone.

She must have known. Those were the last words she said to me. I flew to Chicago two weeks before the High Holidays after she went into a coma. Standing at the bank of phones at O'Hare, I called her hospital room to let someone know I was on my way.

"How is my mom doing?" I asked the nurse who answered.

There was a hesitation. I asked again. "This is her daughter; how is she doing?"

"The family went home," was all the voice on the other end said.

Standing next to her grave two days later, I knelt down and opened the locket on the tombstone next to hers. There was Dad's face smiling at me. I looked at Mom's grave. I smiled, knowing they would be happy finding each other again. I felt warm inside believing they would be celebrating their grandson together. Tears flowed as I rejoiced that we had made peace and reconnected before it was too late.

Just in Time

The jubilant births of Tanner in 1988 and Jamie in 1989 encouraged me to revisit the relationship with my mother and her role as grandmother to our three children.

My mother. I imagined saying the word Mother. I didn't want to refer to her as my *real* Mother. Andi and I shouldn't have to call her Colorado. I wanted to call her Mother, my Mother.

My mother and her husband Bill moved to Vista, California to enjoy retirement and the weather on the coast. How I addressed my mother changed when she and Bill arrived in town to visit his daughter and her family, as well as us. I decided to initiate a belated and much-needed conversation over dinner. On one hand, I was nervous about the possibility of conflict and denial. I didn't want guilt to rear its ugly head and I didn't want any blame placed on me when I approached the topic of the past. On the other hand, I longed for the relief of letting thoughts come forward regarding the strained relationship that had loomed over us for so many years.

I didn't bring Chuck and the kids to this dinner, knowing we needed privacy for the impending conversation. I purposely chose my seat at the Olive Garden Restaurant with my mother sitting in the chair to my left and Bill across the table from me. I wanted to be sure I could look into their eyes almost simultaneously.

I settled in my seat, pretending to scour the menu, but all I could think about were the words I was about to say and my mother's reaction. I had finally mustered the courage to spill my thoughts about what had festered for so long on my mind. The time had come.

After our sodas arrived and we ordered dinner, I looked from my mother to Bill and, with a heavy sigh, found the words to start the conversation. I think they were surprised I had something to say because, most often, our conversations consisted of their barrage of questions and my briefest answers.

"You know," I said directly to them, "life is short. I had nothing to do with the decisions of the past regarding where I lived or who was my mother." I looked directly at my mother and continued. "I am tired of being reminded of your bitterness each time I see you. You talk about what could and should have been. You remind me that you could have taken me back. You don't seem to understand that we don't have a relationship because I wasn't given the opportunity to know you as my mother. To me and all those around me, it was a secret that I was in foster care. Even when I found out and started the court visits with you and Andi, there was still secrecy. I was in the middle, not knowing what to think let alone say to you or my foster parents. I could not ever treat you like a mother because you really never *were* my mother. I can't imagine how that felt to you, but I knew I couldn't allow myself to feel much. The good news is you are happy now and married to a wonderful man. Andi and I are both happy with our husbands and children of our own. Can we just go forward now?"

I was sweating and tore the napkin in my lap as I continually folded it between my fingers.

"I didn't like how everything was handled," she said in a hushed voice.

"I can understand," I responded, reaching for her hand.

Nothing more needed to be said. For the first time, I was able to lean over and hug her without prodding myself insincerely. "I love you, Mother," I said. She pulled her chair next to mine and grabbed me in her arms.

During dinner, I shared details about my new entrepreneurial venture and relished feeling her pride. I had left Group W Satellite Communications and started my own business. I told her all about my first clients and the opportunity to be more available to our kids. She and Bill told me about their life in California. We shared a sweet good-bye as I drove home, excited to tell my husband about my new feelings for Mother. Yes, that's when I started calling her Mother.

Two weeks later, at 8:30 a.m., I whizzed through my office door quickly glancing at the marquis on the wall - Price & Associates. After 16 years of corporate life, I proudly owned my own company providing sales, marketing, production and training services to the telecommunications industry. I recalled how proud Mother was to hear of the new venture.

That morning, I had put down my briefcase just as the phone rang. My assistant said, "Bill is on the phone." The only Bill I knew was Mother's husband. Andi and I recognized Bill as a saint because he lived with Mother's bitterness and supported her with generosity.

Why is he calling me and so early? I asked myself. I sat at my desk and, with trepidation, picked up the blinking line.

"Your mother had a brain hemorrhage last night while we were at Temple," his voice cracked. He was crying. "She's on life support and I don't want to make any decisions until her daughters are at the hospital here in San Diego. The prognosis isn't good." I sat speechless for what seemed like forever.

Recalling our heart-to-heart conversation only fourteen days before, I felt a tremendous void in a place that had only been filled for a short time. I felt so sorrowful for Bill, and I was startled that he wanted Andi and me to make a life-and-death decision for a woman with whom we hardly shared life. I had just started calling her Mother.

"Bill, thank you for being a wonderful husband. I will say a prayer and be in San Diego as soon as I can," I told him. "Thanks, Jackie. Your mom would want you and Andi here," he answered.

As soon as my colleague Susan heard the news, she said without a question, "Get ready, you're out of here," and she made plane reservations. I called Andi who had received the news right before me. She was scurrying to make flight arrangements, too. We didn't say much. We didn't have to, yet. We both knew we were about to step into an experience of responsibility for our mother. The decisions on life-and-death would bring up the thoughts of ifs and shoulds. I wondered what would be different if I had accepted Mother sooner. I worried that I should have had the conversation years ago.

I arrived at the San Diego airport about 5 p.m. the same day Bill phoned. Some of Bill and Mother's friends met me at the arrival gate. They didn't know me, although they knew about me. I didn't know anything about them.

"Thank you for being here. How do things look?" I asked.

"It's a very sad situation, Jackie," said one of the friends. Quickly, my mind had to switch to my other life as Jackie.

During the car ride to the hospital, they told me they had been at a Temple meeting with Mother and Bill when she slumped over mid-sentence. They rushed her to the emergency room.

As we approached the hospital, I felt pains of deep anxiety, loneliness, helplessness and pure nervousness. Bill met me at the ICU waiting room and we embraced in silence as tears enveloped us both.

I approached Mother's room and timidly walked toward her bed. She lay there motionless with a myriad of tubes and blinking machines strung about her shoulders and over her head. I took her hand, and felt broadsided by the realization that she was truly my mother. I finally knew what *real* meant. I was filled with sorrow for the life she was given, guilt for my inability to bond with her in that life, and profound sadness for all the time we had lost. "I'm sorry, I'm sorry," I whispered as the tears flowed and dropped into the hand that held hers. With the rabbi joining me on one side and Bill standing on the other, I turned to Bill, embraced him and shared my grief with him. Then I turned back, taking the hand of my mother - my *real* mother.

Bill and I drove to the airport around midnight to pick up Andi. He kept repeating Mother's final words, "I love my Temple." Maybe it was the Temple that had helped her accept the past. Maybe it was the Temple that comforted her.

When Andi came off the plane, we solemnly hugged without saying a word. We didn't have to. We held each other's hands tightly during the ride to the hospital.

Back in the room where the rabbi continued to honor our mother by staying with her, Andi walked the same path I'd taken toward the bed. She took her hand. Our little family never had a *real* chance to be together in life. Yet here we were, together in death.

I joined Andi and put my arm around her waist. Then she looked at me and said, "I just think she is going to sit up and yell 'Is this what I had to do to get my family together?'" We both muffled a nervous laugh at that sad truth.

The doctor stepped in and explained she was brain dead and fully on life support. Bill looked at Andi and me then, as if asking for approval for the inevitable. Together, we decided to let her slip away peacefully.

We said our good-byes, which for Andi and me were apologies for the burden and bitterness of a true reunification that never happened.

Andi and I cried together with our arms interlocked as we watched Bill say his good-byes. Thank goodness for him. Her husband of twenty-seven years was her knight in shining armor, her stronghold to endure the unending desire to deal with the situation of her children. The three of us quietly walked from the room, turning in sadness with one more good-bye. As sisters, we were saying "good-bye" to Mother. The relationship was so clear and *real* now.

Our drive to the hotel was quiet, though we made intermittent comments thanking Bill for taking care of her. We offered him support and boldly talked about funeral plans. Andi and I prepared ourselves for the most difficult day we'd experience as sisters, not only because Mother would be buried, but also because we would be in a world that didn't belong to us.

Bill's daughter and son flew into the city and each, in separate conversations, told us of their love for Mother and how she loved us so much. They knew her better than we ever did, and I felt badly about that. They had accepted her as a stepmother long ago and shared close relationships with her.

Andi and I walked to Bill and Mother's house from the hotel the next morning to help make the plans for the funeral. We didn't know what to expect of our roles at the memorial service. We agreed we would just do what Bill wanted or what seemed natural - although natural was hard to define on that day.

People started to arrive at their home to pay respects. Andi and I didn't know most of them and wondered what they knew about us. I answered to "Lynn." I answered to "Jackie."

Uncle Lenny, our mother's brother, and his wife arrived with their children from Los Angeles. So did other relatives from New York and California. I vaguely remembered a name, a face, a story, yet they all knew me as Jackie. On one hand, it was uncomfortable to be with distant acquaintances who were relatives. On the other hand, I felt some comfort and unconditional understanding.

The funereal limousine arrived for the immediate family. I just kept thinking, *Lynn, Jackie, or whatever your name is, that's you. You need to get in the car.*

As I stepped from the limousine after arriving at the cemetery, two women standing near a fence caught my eye. With a double take, I realized they were my foster cousins Jill and Jeri from Los Angeles. Their presence seemed awkward. They weren't a part of *this* family.

Confused, I let go of Andi's hand and slipped away toward Jill and Jeri. "What are you doing here?" I asked in a whisper.

"We felt someone needed to keep you grounded," said Jill.

They were thinking for me when I couldn't think for myself. Here I was, living Jackie's life and trying to determine my role. And they understood.

As we approached the gravesite, Andi and I were motioned to the front row. When we walked by the guests, I didn't want to look into any eyes. Someone said, "I'm so sorry." I could only nod my head and say "Thank you." As we waited for the rabbi to start the ceremony, others shared how wonderful Mother was. I just thought, *I wouldn't know.* This certainly seemed like someone else's life and I didn't belong here.

I snapped back to reality as the rabbi eulogized Mother. She read, "The mother of Andre Joy and Jackie Lynn." Bill handed us a poem. "Please read this," he whispered. I silently gasped, feeling that this whole event was happening to someone else, not me. I stood up to face Mother's casket and read the first part of the poem. Andi rose and tried to read the conclusion, then broke into sobs. I took the paper and continued reading with a broken voice, then Andi and I sat down. The rabbi spoke again, telling everyone about our mother as a woman who loved her children and her Temple. I thought, *I hadn't allowed myself to feel that real love.*

We watched her casket get lowered into the ground. The rabbi motioned for Bill, Andi and me to rise and step forward. Bill took the shovel, scooped in some dirt and tossed it into the grave as he heaved loud sobs. It came my turn to pick up a shovel and fill it with dirt. When I tossed the dirt into the grave, I finally cried from the bottom of my heart. I cried for missing out on a life I never knew. I cried for a person who had never succeeded in being the mother she wanted to be. I cried at missing out on a childhood with my sister. I cried for my *real* family.

Back at the house, I listened to everyone tell stories. For two more days, visitors paid their respects. As the hours unfolded, so did the stories. We poured over baby pictures of Andi and me that close and distant relatives had in their wallets or memory boxes. We eagerly watched a video of the *real* father we never knew. Relatives shared stories and discussed the hows and whys of our entry into foster care. "Your father made her crazy," said one relative. "Our family just couldn't take care of you," said another. They spoke of the ways our mother had fought the system and of life events that we never knew.

As Bill, Andi and I went through her personal belongings, he urged us to take some mementos. Our greatest treasure was a two-part ring. We each took one part and felt closer knowing they belonged together, to our mother, as we did. We looked in her closet and found Andi's baby book and more pictures she had hidden away. Now, memories had a whole new meaning.

I had told Mother at dinner, life was indeed short. I had told her just in time.

My Real Father

Fourteen years before Mother's death...

Andi and I didn't ask about our *real* father very often. My foster father Alex was the love of my life as a father and I never wanted him to feel otherwise.

Even with our strained relationship, Andi and I still had an unspoken respect for our mother, so we didn't ask questions about our *real* father. While Mother was alive, she felt that since we never treated her like a mother, we had no business wanting to know or find our *real* father. Outside of screaming about his shortcomings, our *real* father "Harry" was a banned topic.

So without telling Mother, our first letter went out July 8, 1980, to Ms. Louise Dorman at the Jewish Children's Bureau in Chicago. "My sister, Andi and I would like to know the proper procedure to follow in obtaining information about our father and his family," I wrote. Ms. Dorman wrote back stating the agency only knew his name and our parents' date of marriage.

With such little information, plus our hesitation to approach Mother or other relatives, I created a file and put it in my "another time" drawer. Time passed and whenever Harry's name or the concept of father came up with Mother, I heard the same gambler and ladies man story with nothing more to know or pursue.

I caught the "I want to know bug" again in 1984. Because I was recently married, my thoughts about the lack of a father to walk me down the aisle or a grandfather for future children drew my curiosity again. Dad had passed away. Even still, I knew he'd understand my renewed interest.

I sent a letter out to an investigation firm on October 23, 1984. "In a nutshell," I stated, "Andi (born Andre Joy Paul) and I (born Jackie Lynn Paul) were placed in separate foster homes when our mother (Bernyce Paul) had a breakdown and was placed in an Illinois State Institution. From what we know, our *real* father had deserted her recent to that time…All we know is that he is from Chicago and my birth certificate says he was a storm door salesman."

The investigative firm responded with a list of nine Harry Pauls with no or different middle initials around the Chicago area. I trembled with anticipation as I called each one. Rather than ask if there was a Harry Paul who had been married to Bernyce, I simply asked if the Harry Paul was born in the 1920s, the time we concluded according to his age on my birth certificate. The listings came up short. Those Harry Pauls were not our Harry Paul. We continued to work with the investigative firm, turning up prospects based on birthdays and names. We found a Harry with a birth certificate noting parents from Greece. Somewhere along the way, we heard that our *real* father Harry was Greek Orthodox before he converted to Judaism. We uncovered conflicting reports of different social security numbers and a Harry residing in a few different suburbs. We found the marriage certificate and copies of draft papers. We had Harry on paper in historical terms, but not in person. At one point in 1987, the investigative firm identified a doctor with the same name and appropriate year birth date. He was not our Harry.

During a visit with Mother before the birth of my first child in 1986, I asked her once again about Harry. I told her I was curious because I was going to have a baby and while she would be a grandmother, I wondered about my son or daughter's grandfather. Reluctantly, she shared information about his brother Stuart, in the Chicago suburbs. She said she had a wonderful relationship with Stuart, who was equally disappointed with Harry's addictions and subsequent abandonment of us.

She said she and Stuart kept touch over the early years, but the pain of the past caused a disconnect. Then to my surprise she took out her phone book and went right to his phone number. I copied it down and put it in my wallet.

"I'm looking for Stuart," I said to the woman on the other end of the line.

"He's at work right now. Can I take a message?" she responded.

"I'm Lynn and I believe he is my uncle. Is his brother Harry?" I stuttered.

"Yes, his brother is Harry. Is this Jackie Lynn?"

I was startled. She knew me. She explained that she was Stuart's wife and that he would look forward to speaking with me. After a few seconds of silence, I collected my thoughts. *This may be our link to our real father.*

"When would be a convenient time to call back?" I asked.

I grabbed a pad and pencil and picked up the phone to call Uncle Stuart that evening when he returned from work.

"Uncle Stuart, this is Lynn, I mean Jackie," I said to the husky voice on the line.

He cried, literally, as he said, "I have often thought about you and your sister Andre. I've been so disappointed with Harry. Not only did he abandon you and your sister, he abandoned his own immediate family."

I started crying. This man remembered me, yet Andi and I didn't know him. He felt sorry for our loss, which was also his.

Uncle Stuart went on to tell me the last time he saw our *real* father was several years earlier when he borrowed money and never came back. The last time he spoke to him was to let him know their brother died. He hadn't heard anything since and didn't have any contact information. We talked briefly about the early days with his brother and the fun they'd shared. He spoke of another brother with disabilities and Harry's love for him. He shared his hurt for Harry's defiance and denial of his shortcomings. Then I told him all about Andi and me. We decided to meet the next time I visited Chicago.

Several months later, Chuck and I flew to Chicago and drove to Andi's home in Sycamore. There, we anxiously awaited the arrival of Uncle Stuart. Tears and laughter abounded instantly on the front patio at the door. Uncle Stuart hugged me and held me back to look at me, then he hugged me again. He did the same for Andi. His wife was delighted to witness this reunion. So were Andi's husband Bob and my husband Chuck.

Uncle Stuart took our baby photos out of his wallet and cried, "You are blood of my blood." Amazing. Andi and I did not even know this man, and he had our pictures in his wallet.

"Did your family ever think about taking care of us?" I asked later over lunch.

"We were never given the option," answered Uncle Stuart.

"Why didn't we ever see your side of the family?" I continued.

"Your mother kept us away for the most part. From time-to-time, I spoke to her or Aunt Evelyn, but there was concern because, if Harry came back, many people would be looking for him to collect large overdue debt. I wondered about you through the years," he said, wiping a tear from his eye. "Did you know Harry adopted a daughter in another marriage?"

Andi and my eyes opened wide. He continued, "I used to talk to her all the time, but that was long ago. Her name is Marla and she lived in Kansas City."

Andi and I went back home with hopes that somehow we would meet Harry. With this new link to Marla, I stopped the services of the investigative firm and decided to focus on my pregnancy. I'd continue the investigation at a later time.

After Addison was born, I just wanted to dwell on him and not my *real* father. But two years later, with the arrival of my second son Tanner in July 1988, I once again filled my head with thoughts of my *real* father and my childrens' grandfather.

Finding Marla's phone number in Kansas City was not easy. With an additional call to Uncle Stuart, we learned that her husband's name was Joe and we got their last name. I anxiously dialed 4-1-1 and groaned as I heard, "At the request of the customer, this number is not listed." I called some colleagues living in the city and asked if they could check local records to track down a number. This proved successful.

I closed the door in my home office and took a deep breath. I dialed Andi first at her home and put her on hold. Then I dialed Marla and pressed the conference button.

"Is this Marla?" I asked.

"Yes," responded the woman on the other end of the line.

"Marla, this is Lynn Price. I have Andi Andree on the phone as well. We understand we may share a father. Is your father Harry?"

"Yes, he is."

"Do you know about us?" I continued.

"Yes, I do," she offered, "but he didn't talk about you much." She related that he lived in Independence, near Kansas City, but they had had an on-and-off again relationship. She told us he was married and divorced from her mother who was very ill. He worked for a siding company. Harry was grandpa to her kids, although they hadn't seen him in a long time. I asked for his phone number. She explained that since she didn't have a good relationship with him, she wouldn't give us his phone number because she didn't want him to get mad the next time they spoke.

"Will you tell him about our conversation and give him my number?" I asked.

"I will try."

We ended the conversation.

It was tough to wait for the phone call. On several subsequent calls I placed to Marla to ask about her communication with Harry, she claimed she hadn't spoken to him. I also asked about him, but she wouldn't elaborate. It was clear she cared for him and was feeling pain because of their disconnect. Then during one conversation, she shared that she had indeed spoken with him and told him about my calls. She let me know that he wasn't pleased with the news but did take my number. I didn't push Marla because I didn't want to lose this valuable link to Harry.

On a business trip to Kansas City, I checked into my hotel and immediately found the yellow pages in the drawer next to the bed. Finding the listings for siding companies, I called the numbers one by one asking for Harry Paul. On the third call, the receptionist said, "Harry doesn't work here, but could likely be found at another shop." She gave me the number.

I nervously dialed that number and asked for Harry. "He has been on vacation, but may be back tomorrow." I slept restlessly as I thought about meeting my *real* father. I wondered what he looked like and what he would say to me.

The next morning, I handed the taxi driver the address of his company, not knowing if the location was near or far. Anticipating what would happen next was exciting and nerve-wracking all at the same time. The driver pulled up to the trailer for the siding company and I asked him to wait with the meter running. When I walked in to a small reception area, a woman appeared from a side office.

"Is Harry in, please?" I asked, gazing down the corridor to see if I could catch a glimpse of him.

"He didn't come in today. He may not be back from vacation," she offered.

She didn't ask who I was or what I wanted. "Can I speak to one of the managers?"

"Sure," she said as she walked toward a back office.

A gentleman came forward and extended his hand. "I'm Lynn. Can I speak to you a moment?" I asked. He led me to another office. I had come this far, and I wasn't going home without information.

"I'm Harry's daughter." My hands shook and my voice quivered but I stood firmly on my feet. I didn't feel I should explain anything more because I didn't know if Harry ever spoke about Andi and me. "Will you give him something for me?"

"Absolutely," said the man.

I left him a picture of Andi and me and our families, then wrote this note: "You have grandchildren who would love to meet you. Jackie Lynn." I added my home and business phone numbers beneath my signature. The gentleman assured me he would deliver them to Harry upon his return.

Back at my office a month later, my assistant announced into the speaker, "Harry Paul is on the phone." I took a deep, anxious breath and tears welled in my eyes. I had waited for this moment for a long time, but I had pushed it to the back of my mind since my visit to Kansas City.

"This is Lynn," I said softly.

"What did you tell this man?" the voice on the other end asked abruptly.

I knew he was speaking about the man at his office. "I said I was looking for my father." I added, "Are you my father?"

The voice answered, "I will tell you when I meet you. Sometimes I go golfing in Colorado. I will call you when I come. You have a nice family."

I didn't know what else to say. I wanted to ask questions. Yet, I knew I would have to do it his way or lose the opportunity to meet the gambler and the ladies man. I asked for his phone number and he hesitantly gave it to me. "I look forward to your visit," I said. Then he was gone.

I waited for his call week after week. I knew it had taken him one month to place the initial call, but now many months were flying by. Taking the phone number I had placed in my desk drawer, I mustered the courage to call him.

"I'm still looking forward to your visit," I told him.

"I still plan to come and I'll let you know when," he said and hung up.

The visit never came. I pounded my fist on the desk when I tried his number again and heard, "This number has been disconnected." I called the siding business and they told me

Harry had resigned. I went back to the beginning, wondering if meeting my *real* father was meant to be.

Once again, we put the investigation on the back burner until Mother passed away in May, 1994. Andi and I wanted to know the truth behind the gambler and the ladies man; we figured more information might surface with our mother gone. In October 1995, I called and interviewed investigative firms in Kansas City. I wrote letters saying, "I'd like you to help me locate my father whom I have tracked to Independence, MO...

Birthdate:	January 29, 1925
Birth Name:	Harry Andrew Pappas
Changed Name:	Harry Andrew Paul, November 7, 1949
Converted to Judaism:	November 9, 1949
Married Bernyce Brozosky:	November 13, 1949
Entered Service:	June, 1943
Discharged From Service:	January, 1945
Took Off:	Around July 14, 1955
Divorce Papers:	December 15, 1959

...Andi and I don't want anything from him except what most kids want looking for their long lost families - a sense of history and closure. I would like to land on his doorstep."

By January 8, 1996, we engaged a savvy lady by the name of June who had her own investigative firm in Kansas City. Immediately she and her colleagues set their sights on court-house documents, a speculative residence address and surveillance. On thirty-one different days, and several times a day between January and April, the investigators looked for signs of Harry Paul at the residence by calling a phone number or driving by. There was no activity until April 16, 1996, when a car was sitting in the driveway upon the investigator's arrival. The investigator approached the door posing as a lost motorist. A gentleman answered the door, gave directions and then introduced himself by name, Harry Paul.

"We found him," said June excitedly to me over the phone. I gasped for air. I sank in my chair. I couldn't feel my legs. *She found him.* I couldn't believe it. I called Andi. "It is time to meet Harry," I screamed.

On April 24, 1996, Andi and I arrived within minutes of each other at the Kansas City International Airport. After 11:00 p.m., we raced out the door of the terminal. Heading for the rental car bus, we passed a policeman and asked him about driving to the address I had clenched in my hand. He recommended we wait until the morning. We checked into the Doubletree Hotel and spent the night creating scenarios of meeting our *real* father. We looked forward to this reunion with fear and hope.

June picked us up at the hotel at 8:00 a.m. She suggested we go for breakfast so we could meet one of her colleagues who was active on the case and talk about the investigation. We could hardly stand another waiting period, but we were eager to respect the women who led us to a dream. Andi and I sat across from these two striking women, leaning forward and hanging on their every word.

"We are so excited for you," said June.

"Thank you so much," Andi and I echoed. We believed we were about to meet our *real* father.

We finished our coffee and got into their van at curbside. June drove the car to the third level of the parking lot across the street from the restaurant. As we gathered in the back of the van, June pushed a video into the small TV. Before our eyes was the surveillance of the stranded motorist escapade with Harry. *It was him.* While older, he had the features we saw in his younger days from a photo Andi had. "We are ready," I shouted with a nervous laugh. "Let's go!" we all yelled in unison. Andi and I followed the van in our rental car.

The van was positioned on the diagonal corner of the street with the video camera poised to capture our reunion with our *real* father. *What would we call him? Would he close the door in our faces? Would he ask us in?* The car was in the driveway. Andi and I giggled and held hands as we approached the door and rang the bell. No one answered. We called the phone number as the investigators did so often, only to hear a male voice on the answering machine. We didn't dare leave a message.

We waited in the van for hours. We left for lunch and came back, then repeated the walk to the door. No one answered. The investigators had to take a break, so they left us for a while to sit and watch on our own. A few hours later, they gave us a break while we went to grab some dinner. We drove back and repeated the walk to the door. No one answered. We called the phone. The answering machine picked up again.

The house stood on the corner of a busy beltway where one couldn't see the garage from the front door. So we sat in the car and then on the grass across the median, where everything was clearly visible, creating stories of where Harry could be at the moment. As a gambler, maybe he was at the Riverboat Casino or the Royals Game. We had heard he loved to golf so perhaps he golfed all day and hadn't returned yet.

We watched the mail carrier put mail in the box. Andi ran up to ask him if Harry lived there. While he wouldn't say directly, he said the residents usually get their mail every couple of days. We knocked on the neighbors' doors and asked if they knew Harry. They knew Harry, but said they hadn't seen any activity at the house for a few days.

While sitting back on the grass, a gentleman came by and said his wife was about to call the police. He wanted to know why we'd been there all day. We said we were long lost relatives waiting to surprise a family member. Now he was excited for us. If only he knew!

We sat and watched for an entire additional day and returned the next morning knowing that, between sunrise and sundown, it was our last chance to meet Harry during this visit.

Time lingered and as 6:00 p.m. hit, we thought about the 7:00 a.m. planes we'd have to catch back home the next morning. June returned and we put our heads together to make a plan. First, we peered into the garbage can in the backyard and pulled out receipts we found there. On April 4th Harry got an oil change at a service center in Scottsdale. On April 17th, Harry bought gas in Kansas City. On April 20th, Harry got a vehicle inspection in Independence. We surmised he was in Arizona and arrived back in Kansas City in the past couple of days. Maybe he went golfing in Arizona and just got back. We tried to peer into his car sitting in the driveway for any ideas, but we couldn't see much.

Where was he? We went to the mailbox to look at the senders of the mail. The address of a trailer park shined brightly on the upper left corner of one of the letters. We ran back to the car and dialed 4-1-1 on the cell phone. There was a hush as I asked the receptionist for Harry Paul. She said Harry went home a couple of weeks ago, but James was still there. He was out riding his motorcycle.

Andi and I started pacing, deep in thought and shaking our heads from side to side. Then one of us shouted, "What's going on here?" or "Where could he be?" We volleyed questions back and forth, laughing nervously. Harry must have come home to Kansas City. We knew he was with James, whoever James was, in Arizona. But suddenly he bought gas in Kansas City. Where was he?

We called Marla. We were reluctant to call her because we didn't want her to sabotage our meeting with Harry. But, perhaps, she would lead us to him. Maybe he was at her house.

"I don't know where he is. I still haven't seen him in a long time," she said.

We waited another hour and at 7:00 p.m., we called Scottsdale again. James came to the phone.

"Hi, James," I started. "I'm Lynn, a friend of Harry's and I'm in Kansas City looking for him. Do you know where he is?"

"He stays at my home. Try this address and phone number." I listened as he gave me the information for both. Little did he know we were standing outside the home we now learned he shared with Harry and had dialed the number inside all day that answered with a male voice message. But James' suggestion to try his home confirmed Harry was in town.

At 7:45 p.m., Andi and I agreed we weren't going home without meeting Harry. "James, this is Lynn again. Do you have any idea where Harry may be? I'm leaving town in the morning and I don't want to miss him," I said boldly.

"Who are you, really?" he asked.

No more secrets, I thought. "A long lost relative," I answered.

"How long and how lost?" James chided.

"I'm his daughter and it has been forty years," I blurted out as I thought of my age and the span of time since he left.

"Try the medical center. Room 640," James relented.

"Is he okay?" I asked.

"He's got complications," James ended the conversation.

Andi and I looked at each other. "Complications from what?" I shouted into the air.

Like a lunatic, I screamed for Andi to close the door of the car we had opened to get some air. We giggled, shouting nonsense as my mind raced with the close of visiting hours usually at 8:00 p.m. at hospitals. I screeched into a gas station where Andi ran in to get directions. "Few blocks this way and ten blocks that way," pointed the attendant.

We raced out of the car, delirious, nodding to each other with apprehension and excitement as we agreed to be cool, calm and collected when we entered the hospital. We walked briskly through the lobby, took the elevator to the 6th floor and stopped short of his closed door.

"Is Harry taking visitors?" I asked the nurse.

"Let me ask the doctor," she replied loudly without asking who we were. We cringed, fearing he would hear the corridor chatter about his surprise visitors. Andi and I didn't even know why Harry was there, but we acted like concerned family members.

We stopped the nurse from calling for the doctor, but then he came around the corner. "How's Harry?" I asked.

"He's doing okay," answered the doctor.

"Is he taking visitors?"

"Let me check on him first," he replied, pushing open the door to Room 640 and disappearing for a moment. He came out and motioned us toward the open door. "Sure, go on in," he said without hesitation. Then he left without even asking who we were.

Andi and I walked into the room to find a distinguished-looking gentleman sitting on the bed. No machines or pieces of medical equipment were evident. "I don't know you," he said, looking suspiciously from one of us to the other.

"Well, we know you," I said, looking directly into his eyes.

"I don't know you," his voice rose.

"You might know us as Jackie Lynn and Andre Joy. We are your daughters," I said with a quivering voice.

"How did you find me? Get out of here!" he screamed.

Andi stood to the side and a little behind me. I couldn't see her reaction, but thoughts of persistence raced through my mind. We hadn't come this far to leave.

"How did you find me?" he urged again.

"I'll tell you something about how we found you if you tell me something about being our father," my voice demanded. There was silence. Then I took a chance to continue the conversation. "I talked to your friend James."

"Did you tell him who I was to you?" he asked, agitated.

I didn't answer, because I didn't want to lie. I just said, "We believe you are our father."

"I'm not your father," he said emphatically.

"What?"

"I'm not your father," he repeated. "Leave, now!"

I motioned to Andi who started toward his bed carrying a photo album. "Then why is your name on our birth certificates and why are you holding Andi in this picture? Why won't you admit it?" I asked.

"I'm not your father. I couldn't have children," he said, calmly looking at the album.

"Couldn't have children? What are you talking about? Here you are in the picture. You were married to our mother!"

"I couldn't have children," he said, looking down at the album and then handing it back to Andi.

I was silent as a thought bolted into my head repeating his words to myself. *He couldn't have children.*

I paused and the thought continued, *that means…*

"So - you mean artificial insemination?" I could hardly get the words out of my mouth.

"Yes, your mother went to that Doctor Rubin behind my back," he said, his temper rising and his words coming faster. "I was too young to be married. I just left. The marriage felt like pressure."

"But we saw a video of you and me, and you appeared as if you liked me," Andi spoke up.

"I probably did. I liked kids. But I couldn't have kids so I didn't want kids. When she was pregnant with you," he looked over at me, "I couldn't believe it. That was the turning point. I couldn't take that family," he said calmly.

"She pressured me into marrying her. She made me change my name, my birthdate, and my religion. I left my family, too."

"So, why are you hiding?" I asked.

"I hide the past and live for tomorrow," he said matter-of-factly.

"Did you know that after you left, Andi and I were placed in foster care?" I reluctantly asked.

"No."

"Are you very ill?"

"I have tumors on my lungs and vertebrae."

"Did you ever miss us?"

"I didn't want children. You weren't my children, so I didn't miss you," he said.

Andi and I told him about our families and said we would keep in touch. As we walked out of the room, we sensed a lot of sorrow for the man who was our father, married to our mother for eight years, but wasn't our *real* father. How could Mother not give us this information?

As we walked to the elevator, we heard the message come over the loud speaker: "Visiting hours are over." Andi and I looked at each other shaking our heads. "We did it, in time," I said.

Over the next few weeks, Andi and I shared this unbelievable account with relatives. Most of them expressed total denial and responded with "No way."

Bill said, "I thought I knew everything there was to know about your mother, and I've never heard this."

Her brother Lenny said, "This is outlandish."

Aunt Evelyn's daughter said, "This is the craziest thing I ever heard. You would have thought I'd have heard something about this in forty years."

Uncle Stuart said, "He is mental. I don't believe it."

One month later, I sent a note to Harry thanking him for his time, and included a few more photos of Andi and me and our families. I wished him well assuming our paths would not cross again.

"Your mother went to that Doctor Rubin," rang in my ear. I went to the safe deposit box the next week and took out my birth certificate. I looked at the doctor's signature line and read, "Doctor Scott Rubin."

Next, I called my lifetime friend Lane, an attorney in Chicago, and asked if he could find a Doctor Rubin. Only moments later, he called back. He had researched the Medical Society directory and found a practice for this Doctor Rubin.

He called and the receptionist answered, "Fertility Clinic." Lane asked about Doctor Rubin and she said he was long gone. When Lane shared why he was looking for him, she added that if anyone conducted artificial insemination back then, it was most certainly Doctor Rubin as he was a specialist in infertility.

I took the number from Lane and called her back.

"Does 'long gone' mean he passed away?" I asked.

"No, and in fact, he is an adjunct professor at Northwestern Memorial. His practice was sold to the University of Illinois. You should call those places."

Angela in medical records at Northwestern told me Doctor Rubin had retired, but she couldn't give me his number. She suggested I write a letter to him, send it to her and she would deliver it.

I wrote, "Perhaps you can help us solve a mystery, put some pieces of a puzzle together, and ultimately put closure to a situation we've been trying to understand for quite some time…Can you please tell me if you performed artificial insemination around 1954? Was there a sperm bank available? Was it a test…" I included an article from the *Las Vegas Review Journal*, "Missing Person, Woman's Search for Biological Father Only Turns Up More Questions" of July 9, 1996, written about Andi's and my search for Harry after we found him in Kansas City.

I asked Andi to pull out her birth certificate. It noted Doctor Kahn as her delivery doctor. Further reviews showed not only were Doctor Rubin and Doctor Kahn partners, but Doctor Kahn was still practicing in the Chicago suburbs. I sent the same letter directly to him. And then we waited.

Next, I sent a letter to a professor at the University of Illinois who responded, stating that the University of Illinois didn't purchase the practice, but the hospital where I was born had acquired it. He included Doctor Rubin's home address for reference along with a suggestion to contact the hospital. He closed with, "Permit me, however, to wish you the best of luck in the pursuit of your search."

In support of our search, I received a card from Uncle Lenny. "Hang in there. We know you will come out on top." I didn't know what that meant.

I called the hospital. They confirmed that Doctor Kahn and Doctor Rubin were leaders in infertility.

"Well we don't have the records from back then, the program was informal." They suggested the sperm donors were probably young resident doctors where they matched some color traits for insemination.

I called 4-1-1, got Doctor Rubin's home phone number, and called him.

"Is this Doctor Rubin?" I asked.

"Yes, it is," he answered.

"Doctor Rubin, this is Lynn Price. I sent you a letter recently."

"Yes, I have the letter, Lynn. I read your article. Yes, I did artificial insemination back then, but I don't remember your mother and I don't have any records. I can't help you, but I wish you well." I hung up the phone wanting to ask so many questions but didn't know where to start.

Next, I called Information and asked for Doctor Kahn's phone number.

"Hello, this is Doctor Kahn," he said. "I am in receipt of your letter. It is very possible that there was artificial insemination."

"Were we a test?" I asked.

"No, there was artificial insemination back then. People hardly spoke about it, though. Your donor was probably an intern. You are probably genetically better off. That's all I can help you with."

We continued to share information with our biological relatives and Bill, but they still didn't believe any of this. Yet, I knew time was running out. Harry had cancer. He was dying.

I called June and asked her to check on Harry's whereabouts. She confirmed he was still at the medical center. She recommended calling an attorney.

"No matter what he says or does, the law already presumes he is your father," said the lawyer I consulted.

"Andi and I want to know if he our *real* father," I retorted.

"Okay, but we don't require anything from him," I responded. "We just need to know if he is or is not our biological father," I said.

The lawyer provided suggestions including filing a lawsuit to determine heirship and to ascertain if blood work could be obtained for a paternity test.

Three months later, in August, 1996, the first letter was hand delivered to Harry Paul. It read: "They would like to request your assistance in providing a blood sample for testing…my clients are not interested in any financial gain from you or your estate. They simply want a final answer to the issue of their genesis…We understand you are ill and we will make every effort to minimize your involvement in this matter…"

It was the end of August. Harry wouldn't give blood. We pondered whether we should pursue a court order to obtain a sample of his blood.

Then I received a call from cousin Sharon. I had met her at my mother's funeral. She said, "I understand you found Harry and want to determine if he's your father. I've had something on my shoulders for years and I will be so glad to get this out in the open. It's true." Sharon had learned through another relative, that despite Harry's opposition, our mother's wish was to have children *and* Harry, too. So she took herself to the infertility clinic for artificial insemination, not once, but twice.

Our mother went to her grave with the secret of our births.

Andi and I realized artificial insemination more than likely meant we had different fathers. Knowing this only made us feel stronger as sisters. We had embarked on a roller coaster journey into the past, and we wanted some closure in finding out more about our father or fathers.

I even thought about taking out an ad in the *Chicago Tribune*, "Were you an intern during 1954? Do I look like you?"

Of course I never did - and the identities of our birth father or fathers still remain unknown.

Part Two

The Passion of Belonging, Our Campers' Stories

Entrepeneur
and Visionary

Price & Associates was flourishing. An article in the July 2-8, 1993 *Denver Business Journal* hailed my entrepreneurial spirit as *"Marketing Maven Envisions Niche Leading to Fortune 500, Entrepreneur Wowed Her Bankers-Even Without a Business Plan."* It was only the second-to-last paragraph in a two-page feature that referenced a certain stage of my life. *"For Price – who grew up as a foster child in Chicago - success has special meaning. It's a way for her to show that foster kids, who have a certain negative stereotype, can make something of themselves, she said."*

My team at Price & Associates was loyal and my clients trusted the creativity we lent to their sales, marketing and production ventures. I ignited the fuel to ensure business growth through team spirit and camaraderie. My priority embraced my three children who had spectacular sparks of their own. Addison was 5, Tanner was 3 and Jamie was 2. In 1993, I longed to be a "present" mother in light of many years traveling in the cable television programming arena.

Well before starting my own thing, ESPN had been just a few sentences in an article in a sports magazine when I accepted the challenge of putting the network on the television map. My first business card was from Jim Simpson, a sports-caster who exuded positivism and insight. He had placed messages on his business card that mirrored the same. Negotiating four-page programming contracts signed over lunch and eating popcorn in the stands of college football games gave me confidence and fantasies of being the cheerleader of the sports world.

The pitches I created were solid, ranging from taking out an actual softball and throwing it across a client's office to screaming the virtues of this exciting addition to TV programming.

I was also recruited to Group W Westinghouse Satellite Communications and embraced the value of mentoring through working with Roy Mehlman, Harlan Rosenzweig, Don Rasmussen and Jim Bates. They implored me to be highly creative so it wasn't unusual for me to be dancing and singing in my presentations. My clients chuckled when I wore a Mickey Mouse Hat as I spoke about the virtues of The Disney Channel. I wore a Cowboy Hat when I dispelled the myths of the closet country fan for The Nashville Network and a tie when I hailed Wall Street with Satellite News Network. I treasured photos of me with Clint Black and Garth Brooks when they were still new to the music scene. I cherished the opportunity to be an integral member of teams, taking the cable television business to a new state-of-the-art lifetime.

During this time, Andi and I nurtured what we recognized as our special kindred spirit. I invited her to meet me on the road as I traveled by car, bus, plane and train across the country to cable systems in high rise buildings, shopping malls, furniture stores and mom-and-pop homes. I reveled in her ability to inspire me to never take things for granted. She just grinned at the notoriety and business savvy that went with the corporate world I lived in.

In Las Vegas, she came off the plane and spun around laughing like she was Dorothy in the Emerald City with the Wizard of Oz. In Miami, we walked the beach and shared the secrets told by the fortune tellers. In San Francisco, we hiked through the Redwood Forest and chatted along the pier. In Santa Monica, we rode bikes along Venice Beach and cheered on the martial artists performing on the sandy beaches.

Andi usually arrived in the city and registered at the hotel while I was at a business meeting. I looked forward to our reunions with anticipation. By the time I got there, she'd already scoured the literature featuring the history of the facility and the area.

She particularly loved the hotel amenities. When she put her "docsiders" out on the door handle to be polished at the Four Seasons in Chicago, I sobbed tears of laughter as we celebrated our city mouse/country mouse differences with the same heart. We loved our nighttimes, talking across the beds, sharing stories of our youth, still learning about each other's past and the sister moments we never had.

When Roy met an untimely death, I knew the dynamics of management at Group W would change. I had left Group W once during my nine year tenure there. I quickly realized it was a mistake. Roy hired me back when I was seven months pregnant, and moved Chuck and me to Denver from our home in Dallas. Roy was my boss, my mentor, my teammate, my father figure and my friend. Everyone loved Roy with his firm leadership. He received respect for his wisdom, but it was his loving heart that solidified his reputation of being the consummate salesman. Most times, he'd ask "how are you" before "how is the business?" Unfortunately, his cancer spread quickly.

With sadness, I joined several of my colleagues to visit Roy and his wife Gloria toward his final days.

I knew I had to take whatever I learned from him and the other mentors he brought, or shared, at Group W to spread my own wings. I needed to make my own life-balance changes, so I founded Price & Associates. That's how this former youth in care became an entrepreneur. John Sie, the founder of Starz Encore, was my first client. I was running the show and life was glorious for several years.

Glorious, that is, until an even better opportunity presented itself. Chuck received a once-in-a- lifetime career offer in Las Vegas. It meant I could support his good fortune and treat myself and our children to being a full-time mom. Two of my business colleagues stood by ready, willing and able to continue the legacy of my business ventures. I sold the production arm of Price & Associates including Education Showcase, (created with Tricia Dressler and Brian Sullivan) and Top Ten Movie Entertainment (created by Brian and me) to Brian. I sold the Sales and Marketing arm to my dear friend and staffer Susan Burgstiner. It continues to operate today as Marketing on Demand in Colorado. I sold them with trust and pride of my accomplishments. I always wanted to be a full-time mom and was finally able to do that.

While my children were in school, I researched volunteer opportunities that included direct involvement with youth and systemic change. I didn't know the system or the change; I just knew I had to do something powerful "in the trenches" of kids' lives.

Never one to try one thing at a time, I applied for consideration as a Court Appointed Special Advocate (CASA) and a volunteer at Child Haven, a children's shelter. I didn't quite understand why I was drawn to these two labors of love. However, the reasons became clear and bright after meeting the people who welcomed me with open arms. At the time, I didn't understand that I was addressing my past life in foster care by sharing my success with current youth in care. I wasn't bitter; I was happy. I didn't pounce on the system; I honored it. They thought I was bold and courageous; I thought doing this was common sense.

Betsey Sheldon and Jo Ann Angerson at CASA and Peggy Leavitt and Leon Ireland at Child Haven exemplified love in the face of controversy and circumstances in which many become cold and jaded. Children in foster care were becoming my steeds. Until it dawned on me that I had walked in their shoes, I didn't know that the overwhelming nature of giving and receiving would lay footprints on my lifetime memories and bring Andi and I closer together.

My first case included two resilient sisters separated in different homes. I immediately thought of Andi, and realized they didn't understand the impact their disconnect would leave on their futures. I gave them opportunities to value their sisterhood and presented visitation plans with accountability. I urged the judge to approve a biological family reunion, pushing the limits of the position when I presented the case for a trip that would take them out of state. Initially, they wanted to override this celebration with liability and expense. With the judge's agreement, I paid for the plane tickets and spoke about "if only Andi and I had a family reunion." My own kids started to learn the value of sibling relationships and I honored Andi by paying more attention to ours as well.

At Child Haven, the smells of the babies in care comforted me in a way I hoped was mutual. I rocked them gently in my arms in the cottage rocking chair. I placed them in their swings and knelt down to eye level, giggling "weeeee" as I pushed them softy. I tested the temperature of the bottle on my wrist and even tasted the cereal before scooping the food in their anxious mouths. I cleaned their diapers, lovingly referred to as dooty bombers, and rubbed their backs. I sang in a whispered tone "You Are My Sunshine" in their ears as I had with my own kids.

Once a week, we filled each other up with so much love. No matter what their stories, Leon taught me to accept them unconditionally and touch them for the entire time they were in my arms.

Leon was like a smiling teddy bear and, while the infants seemed to disappear in his big arms, he exemplified the leadership skills of reality in doing our job because we had to…and loved to.

There was no doubt I wanted to solve all their family problems. I felt for them intensely and, each week, I took one more loving look as I stepped out the door. I hoped they would leave the cottage to go back home or into other permanent placement, yet I savored the time together if they remained when I returned. Peggy, the director, was there when I signed in at Child Haven, and Peggy was there when I signed out. She always shared a smile of understanding, appreciation and gratitude, validating my reason for sharing the Child Haven family week after week.

One day, the elementary school girls' cottage needed some help, so I walked next door to the innocence of smiles and the chatter of little-girl conversations. As I sat at the courtyard table, I followed the eyes of one of the youngsters to a little boy on the other side of the lawn. "Do you know him?" I asked.

"He is my brother," she answered proudly. "He lives in the cottage over there."

At that moment, a light bulb went on. I thought about my CASA girls and their separation. I watched the brother and sister gaze at each other across a courtyard. I related to their separation and their unspoken bond of connection with thoughts of Andi prominently in my mind.

What can I do to ensure these brothers and sisters share time together in their childhood?

Andi and I had missed out on so much.

The sure bet about foster care is that, one day, we will journey out of the system. That is why I felt a need, a calling, to motivate them to nurture their own identities, destinies and connections. I wanted to encourage foster parents to foster sibling families. I also knew I had to bring these brothers and sisters childhood memories to set the foundation for their conversations and their scrapbooks when they reconnected as adults. I didn't want them to use their journey in the system as an excuse to follow in their parents' footsteps. I knew that stereotypes went with the term "foster child" pushing kids ten steps back before they had the chance to take even a tiny step forward.

After all, some statistics painted a sad picture of foster kids who die prematurely, end up in prison, live on the streets and barely finish high school. Andi and I didn't let the system get us down. Individually and with our support teams, we finished high school, graduated college, mastered careers and celebrated our own families. We found our own friendship and our own sisterhood with, and without, the memories of our childhood together. These kids could have all that we have...I needed to show them, and the nation, they deserve to belong!

In March, 1995, I flew to Chicago to attend the Bat Mitzvah of my girlfriend Audree's daughter. Perhaps it was a coincidence that Audree was the first friend I had told about Andi because as I stood on a stairwell taking in the joy of the celebration, I overheard Audree's sister Eydee talking about her labor of love in Springfield, Illinois. Camp Care-A-Lot was an outstanding camp for children who were underprivileged.

That's it. I'll have a camp for brothers and sisters! I started my mental note pad.

I met Andi at the food court at O'Hare Airport before my return home. She had driven from her home to share time with me before I ventured back home to Las Vegas after the Bat Mitzvah events.

"What do you think about a camp for brothers and sisters who are separated in foster care?" I asked.

"I've never heard of it before, but if you say it's going to happen, it will," she replied.

My greatest fan, my sister, just put more sparks on the fire. How great it felt to belong to her. Camp To Belong. I loved belonging to my sister. *Everyone wants to belong*, I thought.

I introduced Camp To Belong to my CASA colleagues who met the idea with non-hesitant hails of "Count me in." I shared the momentum of this idea with Peggy and Leon at Child Haven and their grins exuded a "go for it" message.

I envisioned what a camp experience would look like, feel like, taste like, smell like and sound like. While camp settings were hard to come by in Las Vegas, the University of Las Vegas offered not only a convenient location, but also an educational environment.

The University's summer program director Tony applauded the idea of bringing siblings together, stating, "I never thought about kids being separated. Let's make it happen."

In March, 1995, we signed a contract for the first Camp To Belong Summer Camp. It would take place in only a few months. I hit the ground running, filing government paperwork for non-profit status and creating a board of buddies who exuberantly took their roles as officers and committee chairs. We brought our entrepreneurial spirit and love of the unknown to go beyond logical strategic planning. If we didn't know something, we found out about it. If we couldn't find out about it, we made it up. "What ifs" turned into "will bes." Hurdles turned us into gymnasts. There was a method to the madness and I was blessed with a team open to "we can do this and do it now!!"

At this time, Terry Prince was my personal trainer whom I trusted to help me gain weight and tone my muscles. Each day, I took a class or worked my upper or lower body with Terry. Little did I know that while Terry's coaching was spectacular for my weight training, it was my mind training that he enhanced with every visit. Between each repetition, I spilled my ideas. As he redirected my thoughts to the machines or the free weights, he cheered on the ideas and spurred on the actions. Terry was also a singer/songwriter and I approached him with several lines of lyrics for a potential camp theme song. In a matter of days he completed the lyrics for "To Belong" and added the music.

Andi also listened to every kooky idea I presented. While she played the devil's advocate from time to time, she never ever questioned the intention, the possibilities, the opportunities or the method to my madness. With her passion and skill as a special education teacher, and an exceptional one at that, she shared her thoughts of the triumphs and challenges with children in an unselfish, unconditional, non-judgmental and purely accepting way. For every conversation in which I said, "We…do this and that," she would say, "This is not we, this is you doing this…stop giving me the credit. Give me the dates and I'll be there."

Chuck knew I was on a mission; he could only shake his head and grin, knowing that I would make this happen.

Okay, so we had a location. UNLV, here we come. We had volunteers calling on their friends to create the experience based on my vision. They would jump in as counselors. We had the professional support from my CASA and Child Haven colleagues. And I had Andi, Chuck and my children for personal support.

We had to raise money and everyone laughed at me when I said, "Don't worry, it will be there. Even if I have to put it in," which Chuck and I did the first year. We pooled our friends and had a kick-a-thon at a martial arts studio to raise money and awareness of this labor of love. We had all kinds of ideas for activities and called on people and places to schedule memorable moments.

But, what about the campers? I approached Stuart Fredlund, the director of the Department of Children and Family Services for Clark County, Nevada.

"Good morning Mr. Fredlund, thanks for taking the time to see me," I said with confidence. I was thrilled he had agreed to meet with me and I knew he couldn't say no to Camp To Belong. *Or could he?*

"I understand you have an idea to share," he responded, inviting me to sit at his conference table.

I talked fast. I thought the faster I talked, the quicker he would realize that I knew what I was doing. Then he'd give me his blessing and lead me to the door.

"Camp To Belong, because everyone wants to feel like they belong, is a special place to bring brothers and sisters together for events of fun, emotional empowerment and sibling connection.

My sister and I were separated. I didn't even know about her until I was 8. Never gave her the time of day til I was 16. Now we are best friends. I don't want kids today to miss out on what we did. Got a place. Got volunteers. Just need your kids." I took a breath.

"Where will the camp be held."

"UNLV."

"Who are your volunteers?"

"Lots of my CASA buddies…you know they are all cleared to work with children."

"What are you going to do?"

"Fun things for them to share."

"Let me talk to my caseworkers."

I ran to the car as fast as I had spoken to Mr. Fredlund. He would find the kids!

In the summer of 1995, Camp To Belong was ready to welcome our first family of siblings.

Our 32 campers started to walk through our doors. While we naturally wanted to extend open arms, we valued the many ways kids would respond to our welcome. We knew that some didn't honor or trust hugs as we did, so we offered a handshake, a high five or a nod. And when we felt comfortable in our own guts, we would say, "Can I give you a welcome hug?" Each child looked at us as they glanced around the lobby to find their brothers and sisters. It was a new experience for everyone; we all were giving it a chance.

Some of our volunteers thought the campers would run into each other's arms with excitement. We learned quickly that reconnections came with hesitancy, but also the benefit of the doubt. Maybe one of the children had called 9-1-1, upsetting his or her sibling. Maybe one of the older children served as the parent to the younger sibling and the younger sibling harbored anger feeling abandonment. Maybe one sibling was placed in a group home while another was the only foster child in a home. Maybe one was in therapeutic care while the other was in a "regular" family. Maybe they had different fathers and were placed with different paternal relatives. Maybe one of the children remained with mom or dad while the other was in foster care. Maybe they had their own secrets and didn't know what they could share with each other. Walls had been built up because of the anticipation and the unknown. We realized it would take time to bring those walls down.

We also realized that some care providers didn't know the other sibling(s) or their respective support teams. Some of the kids had different social workers.

Some questioned our intention. We accepted the reality that the campers needed to build up trust for Camp To Belong.

We saw potential in each of our campers as they arrived at Camp To Belong Summer Camp, had their pictures taken, accepted their Camp T-shirts and stood beside their siblings. We knew all brothers and sisters had the potential to accept their *real* siblings and to eventually feel like they belong.

Their stories follow...

Not Ready for Freedom

Randy had the world by a string. Turning eighteen, he'd become emancipated from the system and officially on his own. The U.S. Marines had beckoned him to join its family.

With the gate to an independent life flung wide open, most people thought he would be sprinting, even high jumping, over to the other side. However, he wasn't ready to walk through the gate, let alone jump over it. He yearned to take his two younger sisters with him.

Randy's younger sisters' participation at Camp To Belong Summer Camp was a given. Laura and Amanda lived in two separate foster homes. The distance and time between visits posed a real challenge to their sisterhood. They missed sharing their everyday lives and greatly anticipated spending a week together. Camp To Belong Summer Camp was eager to welcome these sisters from California to its new site in the Colorado Rockies.

Randy's former social worker supported the young man's desire to join his sisters at summer camp. But because he was emancipated, we had to discuss special considerations. To qualify for attendance, campers needed to be currently living in separate foster homes or other out-of-home care. We had to discern the reasoning and fairness of giving him a slot at Camp while other sibling groups met all the qualifications.

We questioned what Randy would truly gain from summer camp. He could have his "free in the world" hat on with momentum to move on beyond the system. The potential confusion in his role as a big brother, a camper (and the oldest camper at that), and a legal adult needed to be addressed.

In reality, all we needed to hear was how he yearned to be reunited with his sisters through our Summer Camp. They hadn't spent quality time together since he was thirteen. It seemed curious that a teenage male would even want to spend time with his little sisters, especially when he could spend his last days as a civilian hanging out with the boys. We were honored, impressed and eager to meet the young man.

Since I made the rules, I decided I could bend them and allow Randy to come to camp with his sisters.

It was the right decision. Tears brimmed from Randy's eyes as his sisters ran into his arms, tears symbolic of the pain they felt from the past five years of separation. The silence that first engulfed them quickly evolved into a warming chatter. Each vied for the other's attention, locking eyes, huddling close and sharing their stories. Whether the words spilled from their lips or their body language spoke for itself, it was evident the three shared an unconditional love. From the moment of being reacquainted, they were joined at their hips.

Randy instinctively took the role of big brother and never questioned his place as a camper as well. He looked after Laura and Amanda, and they looked up to him. With every activity, they cheered each other on and celebrated everlasting moments of fun.

Petrified of horseback riding, Randy stoutly stated he would pass on this activity. We invited him to come to the stable and hang out in the corral as his sisters donned their helmets and met their horses, which were assigned to match their personalities and experiences. Honest about his fears, he continued to resist the urges to join the trail ride.

Then Laura asked him to go horseback riding. Without a moment's hesitation, he jogged over to the stable and strapped on a helmet. Fear shined in his eyes, but he knew he was needed. With supportive grins from those around him, he jumped on a horse and fell in line behind the girls in his life. He mustered a grin as he stroked the horse's mane and then gave a thumbs up to each of his sisters.

The soon-to-be Marine surprised us again with the way he lovingly sewed, stuffed and decorated a pillow for his sisters. The Signature Sibling Pillow event invites brothers and sisters to create a special pillow for each other to take back to their homes. Campers hug those pillows tight and remember their siblings when they go to bed at night, or simply when they yearn for a sense of closeness with their brother or sister.

Randy, Laura and Amanda all crafted pillows scrawled with messages of love and appreciation that evoked wet eyes and tight embraces during the special dinner event and presentation. Laura read to Randy, "I love you. When you're gone, I cry at night. I wish you were home. Spending time with you makes me feel so good."

I reveled in Randy's ability to not only be a big brother, but also to be a role model for other young men at summer camp. He encouraged their love for their siblings and their potential success beyond being in the system. We had many a heart-to-heart talk of reciprocal admiration.

Randy was a vibrant youth who could belt out silly camp songs, conquer his fears and sensitively reveal his emotions. Tears streamed from his eyes at the closing campfire, knowing the time with his sisters had drawn to a close. He stirred us by inspiring others to cherish their sibling connection; he moved my heart with his respect for the opportunity to come to summer camp and his zestful leadership. He spoke highly of his foster parents, shining a light for other campers to follow by honoring their relationships, even though it hurts to divide parental loyalties. His presence illuminated every camper and counselor. And his sisters felt like princesses graced by a brotherly king.

A few days before, he had been a stranger. Before long, he was a dear friend by every virtue of our unspoken closeness. I made a commitment to stay in touch with Randy's sisters when he entered the service and to share my pride in his bold dedication to his sisters and country.

The girls and Randy took turns giving each other hugs followed by a big group hug. With them, Randy, Laura and Amanda secured a bond of connection for the future.

As Randy lit out for his Marine base the morning after his return from summer camp, he called his former social worker and cried about the virtues of Camp To Belong. He was out of the system, yet he felt strongly that other separated siblings should have what he called, "The best week of my childhood." In reality, it was the *last* week of his childhood. Now he was a man.

Randy remained connected to the place and the people who had so touched him. Soon after summer camp, he wrote me a thank you letter on military letterhead. On Thanksgiving, he called the office from his post in Japan to say thanks for what Camp To Belong meant to him and his sisters.

The following summer, we invited Randy, Laura and Amanda back to the Camp To Belong Summer Camp family.

It was a bittersweet invitation since the girls were still living in separate foster homes. However, we were eager to celebrate the trios reunion again.

Unfortunately, Randy was unable to get leave from the Marines, but the girls came as proud sisters. They recalled their fond memories of the previous summer and the infrequent moments they shared since we'd seen them last. The Camp To Belong family saluted Randy and felt assured that the memories created between his sisters at this summer camp would spill over to their brother through the packages we sent him.

An amazing thing happened next. At the start of the new year, Randy had to request the dates of his next military leave. He didn't have any specific plans; he just craved going home. His first and second requests were turned down. His third request coincided with the next Camp To Belong Summer Camp. Without hesitation, he joined the ranks of our first Counselor In Training Program created for former campers. A Marine taking a leave to serve as a summer camp counselor proved to be an overwhelming compliment to Camp To Belong and an enthusiastic honor to his sisters. At this camp, his sisters, once again, never left his side.

Randy was a full-fledged counselor each summer after that, scheduling his leave to be at Camp. He stands as a courageous beacon of hope for teens in the system who are dismissed as self-centered, non-emotional, non-caring and non-changing with intense readiness to jump over that gate to freedom. He shares how he uses his self-esteem and his voice to create success. He stands proudly as a role model for the significance of the sibling bond as he speaks of his love, memories and connections with his sisters. He stands proudly for

Camp To Belong and the value of its experience in his life, willingly sharing his gratitude.

He also stands proudly in his Marine uniform when he speaks to our teens at the Signature Life Seminar Program and shares the potential for a happy, secure and successful future.

Randy exudes the spirit of the benefits of taking a pause before he stepped through the gate, to sprint farther than we all can imagine. During a recent visit to San Diego, I left word for Randy that I would be in the area of his Marine base. As I finished packing my bags for the airport to return home, the hotel room phone rang.

"I'm downstairs in the lobby," said Randy. I wasn't surprised. I just knew I would see him before I went home.

After an eighteen-hour post, Randy and three of his Marine buddies drove to town and were standing in the lobby declaring they were my chaperones to the airport. Each extended a hand for a handshake, but hugs ensued. I was overwhelmed that they took the time to honor their fellow soldier and me with their visit.

Because I had time before I needed to check in for my flight, we headed to the beach and walked the shore, talking about life. Randy's buddies allowed us time alone as we perched on a huge rock with waves lapping at its base.

Randy had applied for custody of his sister Laura. He talked about his continued quest to gain custody, his concern for Amanda and her transition beyond the system, his love for his foster family, his commitment to the Marines and his dedication to Camp To Belong. In all of his life challenges matching the ebb and flow of the waves before us, the triumphs anxiously made the tides rise. I was overcome with emotion learning the place Camp To Belong held in his heart. He was certainly moving forward, yet he didn't hesitate to look back, share gratitude and give back.

Later, as I stood curbside at the airport and hugged each of them good-bye, I turned around and saluted them. We all understood.

Randy served in Operation Iraqi Freedom and couldn't come to Camp the next summer. What a blessing to receive words of promise, purpose and hope from Randy. "What can I do for you?" I asked over the phone as Camp was approaching.

"Keep giving the other children the experiences you have given me," he said. "Look out for my sisters, too."

His sister Amanda was on her own and unable to attend Camp. I had made a promise to Randy to take care of his sisters. But Laura wouldn't have a sibling present so I bent another rule. We honored Laura at Camp. She initiated another definition of siblings. She joined another former camper whose three siblings had been adopted and therefore could not attend Camp. Together they were Camp To Belong Sisters. They experienced sisterhood and belonging in a special way reserved for former individual campers who need siblings when their own can't be there.

Randy called Laura from his post while we were at Camp. I was standing by her side when she took the phone.

"Hi, I miss you," Laura said with tears running down her cheeks.

She handed the phone to me.

"Thanks for keeping your promise," Randy said.

I hung up and hugged Laura. We were there for Randy, too.

Freedom extended beyond the system, to his sisters and to his country. We witnessed a gate opening for all of us.

Honoring Past Bonds

Why is 6 scared of 7? As the childhood riddle goes, it's because 7 8 (ate) 9. "Illogical!" cries Rick, staunch defender of reason. "It is 10 who should be frightened!"

"And why my brother is right is because if 7 just 8 (ate) 9, then 10 should be more afraid of 7 than 6! Because... 10 is next! Seee-eeee; I told you my brother was smart!"

With this exaltation, the two radiantly blue-eyed boys collapsed into giggles. Jerry stretched his arms up to Rick's shoulders and they tumbled into mock wrestling as easily as they united in a scholarly deconstruction of this time-worn joke riddled with faulty logic.

Arriving from his adoptive home in Illinois, 12-year-old Jerry was never more than a side-step away from his 16-year-old brother Rick at Camp To Belong Summer Camp. Rick lived in a foster home in Virginia and the brothers had seen each other only once or twice annually for the past three and a half years.

"Remember when I was shy last Christmas?" asked Jerry.

Rick smiled, "Yeah, we went out to eat and you were quiet. We hadn't seen each other in a long time."

"You looked really different," said Jerry.

Rick laughed, "I used to be fat."

Like lightning, Jerry jumped to his brother's defense. "You weren't fat! Just baby chubby."

Rick grinned at his younger brother. "When we both lived in Illinois, Jerry and I looked a lot alike. When I saw him here at camp, I was surprised at how much taller he'd grown," Rick paused, "and I realized how much I miss him."

As balmy days burned into crisp mountain nights, every moment from the first one Rick and Jerry shared at Camp was invoked with a sweetness and light that heartened everyone nearby. With a spaghetti-sauce-rimmed smile at Camp's first dinner, Jerry announced to his table, "Did you know that my brother is going to be a famous scientist when he's older? He's really smart and studies physics."

Rick looked at Jerry, placed his arm around his shoulders and nudged his head toward him. "I love my brother," Rick boasted. Jerry's smile in response outshined the sun.

The brothers honorably defended their raft-mates from splashers. They boastfully rappelled down a 75-foot cliff while each excitedly praised the other using new nicknames. Rick grinned as he explained, "When we lived together, I always called Jerry 'Bugs'… after the bunny."

They shared the blazing hot springs pool where Jerry mastered his 720-degree twist double flips off the diving board, while Rick, his biggest fan, cheered wildly from the side.

"Awesome!" he shouted, clapping his hands high over his head.

With elaborate detail and concentration, they choreographed pass, dive and dunk strategies in daring junctions at the pool's diving board and basketball goal, then later squelched the post-swimming shivers by sharing a beach towel.

They created memories of Rick's dogged pursuit to secure Jerry his share of s'mores at the first campfire. Jerry's eyes sparkled each time his older brother confided in him or carried him piggyback. All those around them witnessed their amazing bond.

Memories also lingered of the unabashed affection with which Rick hugged Jerry good-bye as he left to attend the Camp To Belong Life Seminar one morning. Their laughter resonated as they wound their way through Mad Libs® on the bus ride to rock climbing. Unforgettable was Rick's expression as he read the sibling pillow Jerry crafted. It expressed his love and wish that they could see each other all of the time.

The two brothers shared tears and hugs while singing the powerful Camp To Belong theme song, *To Belong*, played during dinner one evening. Fierce solidarity shone through teary gratefulness and grief as they clung to each other at the final campfire.

The image of an ideal sibling bond stood before us. Even in unspoken communication, the two shared symbiotic understanding. Their bond inspired counselors and campers alike, while their contagious, ever-present smiles and saint-like personalities united those present in an aura of ease and acceptance. Rick and Jerry were natural leaders. Both their peers and their counselors at Camp were touched by their magnetism.

"I wish our older brother could have come, too," Rick said. "Someday, I hope that we can all share an apartment together; that is a dream I have," he continued.

Until then, we weren't aware they had another brother. We gave the boys an opportunity to talk about Nate, who was living in another foster home in Illinois. They smiled as they shared stories about him.

Even the most brilliant sunsets fade into dusk, and our luminous Camp regrettably, inevitably, had to end. Rick and Jerry, in a moment of reflection, both showed their gratitude at having had the opportunity to attend Camp. Their favorite part?

"Being together!" said Rick.

"Seeing my brother!" piped Jerry.

Both resolved to stay in contact through the year. Both spoke of their desire to return to Camp, and one day become counselors.

As final boarding calls at the airport beckoned, Rick hesitated to make his way toward the Virginia-bound plane. Down the corridor, Jerry would soon board his plane for Illinois. In their last moment together for what might be an entire year, the boys embraced.

"I love you," said Rick through tears.

"I love you, too," Jerry responded to his big brother.

Across hundreds of miles, they flew to their respective homes while the ache of separation, tempered by memories of the experience, glowed in their hearts and minds. I hoped their recollections whispered of a time when pure happiness, security and love - the pillars in this place of unconditional belonging - were shared together at Camp To Belong.

The next summer, the first part of Rick's wish was fulfilled. Their older brother Nate joined him and Jerry at Camp. Nate's infectious smile and selfless grace was instantly recognizable in his resemblance to his younger brothers. When presenting their sibling pillows, Nate told his youngest brother that despite Jerry's adoption and last name change, "You'll always be a Johnson to me."

The love these three demonstrated with every breath is a source of inspiration stretching far beyond the boundaries of the everyday. Its inner glow blazes brighter with each moment spent in their company, and was evidenced in the letter Nate sent me after Camp. He didn't express bitterness for the summers he missed with them; he only shared gratitude for having the time to catch up with them. We'll always remember these brothers and recognize the inspiration such an unconditional love instills. Here is Nate's letter:

Dear Lynn,

How are you doing? Remember me? It is Nate. I was at camp this past summer and I was thinking about the fun I had at camp, and I wanted to write you. I don't want this letter to be about how much of a wonderful person you are because I am sure that your hear it often enough. (Well what the heck, "Lynn, you are a wonderful person.") I am just so grateful that there are people like yourself who decide to help children who share the disposition that you experienced. I would also like to thank you for inviting me to camp, I had a fabulous time, and I hope when summer rolls around, I once again join the family that you have admiringly established.

When times are hard and I need a brother to cry with or wrestle with, I know that they are not always available. Although this is true, I rest assured knowing that when summer comes, my brothers will be there for me, and that is because of you and your hard work and dedication. When I go to camp, I feel free from the stresses of the outside world and I fall into an endless bliss of love and happiness with my siblings and my peers. Most of all, I would like to thank you from the bottom of my heart because I know that my happiness is brought to me by you and your sister. So even if you have heard thank you a million times today, I just want you to know that as long as I am around, the thank yous will never stop coming!!!!!!!!!

Thanks for everything
With love, Nate

The next year, Rick and Nate returned to Camp To Belong, Rick as a Counselor In Training and Nate his proud little brother. Jerry couldn't join his siblings. We celebrated Rick's high school graduation and his impending move back to Illinois to live with Nate and their biological mother.

Maybe the wish for the apartment will happen some day, too.

Our Dad
is Coming Back

They were a handful, individually and collectively. The four siblings cheered out loud in sudden bursts one by one and all together. They threw their arms up to the sky. The adults were in a quandary trying to decide if they should whisper, "shhhhhhhhh," or if they should shout, "turn up the volume!" and join them with cheers and waving hands. They tickled each other and played pranks. One brother hid another brother's hat and one sister sat on a pinecone placed in the sand by another sister. They laughed at each other's jokes and didn't mind who was the center of attention at any given moment.

They ran in circles around each other and played "monkey see, monkey do" as they grabbed the rings of the monkey bars and jetted from one bar to the next. They pumped-kicked high on the swings and stretched their feet out as far as they could, just to show they could go higher than the others did. They looped their legs and arms through the big rings of the jungle gym, turning upside down and sideways in an effort to link their bodies and not fall in the make-believe swamp below.

From the outside looking in, we saw that, despite their outward display of happiness and confidence, these kids lived in a jungle of sadness and fright.

Cindy, 10, Aaron, 9, Annie, 8 and Dennis, 7 lived at the same address on a children's group home campus. However, they lived in separate cottages where they made their own beds, ate their meals and did their homework with other children of the same gender and age. House parents lived in each home and consistently shared their lives with the children under the same roof, especially in the evening. Even though daytime staff came and went from each home, the brothers and sisters didn't share the same roof, day or night.

Though separated only by courtyards, they couldn't see each other every day. Their daily routines and other activities were scheduled by gender and age. Yet, that didn't stop them from screaming a bellowing hello and waving a hearty good-bye as they traveled across the campus walkways.

These four siblings got invited to Camp To Belong Summer Camp because of their incredible Court Appointed Special Advocate (CASA) Linda, who believed in the significance of their sibling bond. She yearned to give them childhood memories together. With the support of their own social worker Cheryl, the kids packed their bags for the first annual Camp.

The boys ran and jumped. They used their outside voices inside. They egged each other on. They squabbled and shared a few quiet moments. They whispered. They gave each other high fives. They hugged. The girls danced and chatted. They painted their fingernails. They squabbled and made loud noises. They gave each other piggyback rides. They hugged. They "got it" when they did not realize they were "getting it." They were brothers and sisters. At times they got along great, and at other times, sibling rivalry took over.

At Camp, they shared days in a row under the same roof. Given this opportunity, they formed a family. Aaron looked out for Dennis and Cindy looked out for Annie. The boys looked after the girls and the girls looked after the boys.

In sacred moments, they came together and spoke about their absent father, even to the entire Camp To Belong family, with smiles of remembrance splayed across their cheeks. "Our Dad is coming back," was their mantra. They believed, and we believed with them.

So perhaps it was fate when my husband got transferred from Las Vegas to Denver and our family planned a move to the Rockies. "Lynn, we've located Mr. Joe Smith, the father of Cindy, Aaron, Annie and Dennis in Denver. How would you feel about visiting him?" asked Cheryl.

Having the credentials as a CASA myself, and with the support of Linda, I recalled the children's belief in their father and didn't hesitate to prepare to make their dream come true. After all, he said he was coming back for them. Maybe I could help him find his way.

With my first glimpse into Mr. Smith's eyes, I saw the resemblance of all four of his kids. He shook my hand solidly, covering one with the other. I pulled him close for a hug, whispering, "This is from your wonderful children."

When his trusting eyes met mine, I assumed he knew I was not there to judge, but to reunite a family. We sat next to each other on the navy blue couch with the sunlight streaming through the window over our heads. He introduced his nephew and his nephew's wife. They walked into the room smiling and welcomed me into their home. A young great nephew and great niece ran into the room, grabbing the knees of their parents as they hid half way behind their backs. After a few peek-a-boo moments, they were running around all over again, making all of us laugh out loud. They ran into and out of Uncle

Joe's lap, and his love for them was obvious from the tight hugs they shared.

Happily, there was no tension to be broken. I entered the home of a family and immediately knew their cousins would also feel welcome here. The extended family asked about Cindy, Aaron, Annie and Dennis with excitement. I shared with them the children's belief that their Dad was coming back.

They may have been ready for me to unload a bunch of questions including "why" and "how dare you" and "where have you been?" with a cavalry of defense stories ready to be released. I didn't say anything before Mr. Smith offered, "I made some mistakes in the past."

I motioned my hand from side to side, signaling for him to pause. "We've got the future ahead of us," I said. "Tell me about you now." The past obviously had some challenges. In this moment, I was all about the present and future.

"How are my children?" he asked with a tear running down his cheek. "I miss them," he added, cradling his face in his hands.

"They are exceptional. They love you deeply. They say you are coming back for them," I shared softly while moving even closer and taking his hand in mine.

I showed Mr. Smith photos of the kids at Camp. We giggled at their silly stories and at kids being kids.

"I just couldn't be a father," he said, glancing at the pictures. "I needed a job and the help of my nephew and his family."

I nodded my head with understanding.

"Their mother went her own way. I was scared I would falter in her absence."

He didn't realize his absence would send his children into a journey in the system. Yet, like the children, he lived his promise every day, building a stable foundation to bring them home.

He pulled out his old, faded pictures from his wallet and we compared those of his children's faces of the past to those of the present. He shook his head from side to side, smiling and commenting how they'd grown so beautifully.

I reported back to Cheryl. "There are regrets of the past. Yet, everything shows me the future is bright."

Before long, we got the nephew's house ready for the children's home-coming, ordering rental beds and dressers to fill the rooms to be shared with their cousins. Friends brought over clothes and toys. Their young cousins were told they'd have more friends to play with in the house.

Balloons for a welcome home party lined the ceiling and streamers hailed from the light fixtures. A big, brightly colored WELCOME HOME sign shouted from the entrance of the house.

Mr. Smith and I rode silently to the airport. In the terminal, I watched him peer at the airplane as it taxied to the gate. I stepped up to take the balloons and sign he was clenching, realizing he would want his hands free to feel his kids for the first time in a long time. I stood by his side. "Savor this moment," I whispered.

The door opened to the jetway and we moved our heads left and right. I was on tiptoe looking anxiously for the children. Within moments, they were engulfed in their Dad's arms as nervous laughter punctured the air and vibrant tears cascaded. They ran up to me, too, and I was overcome with the significance of being a trusted participant in this amazing reunion.

Then I approached Cheryl who accompanied them to their father's home. We didn't have to say anything. Our trust in one another and the system spoke for itself in the faces of four children and their father. Cheryl hugged each of the children and got back on the plane to return home. The kids really were staying.

"We told you he would come for us," said Cindy, jumping into her father's arms.

I drove Mr. Smith and his children home. Each kept talking at the same time, eager to add to a story or tell their own. I looked in the rearview mirror at the grinning kids clamoring for attention. Then I peered over to Mr. Smith whose smile shined so brightly in the passenger seat as he craned his neck to look with pride at the zesty souls in the back. The kids eloquently displayed their unconditional love by asking what he'd been doing, not where he'd been. "We knew you were coming back for us," they shouted in chorus.

They couldn't believe all the decorations were for them. Their aunt and uncle scooped them in their arms as their cousins shyly shared hellos.

They stood by the welcome cake and I took a wide-smiled picture of this reunited family. It was as if they'd been together forever and were just celebrating another birthday or holiday. The kids smiled naturally. Seeing them share their dad's lap caused a closeness felt by everyone in the room.

And then, as I said my good-byes and embraced them tightly, Cindy grabbed Annie's hand and started singing our Camp To Belong song. "To belong to a loving family...to belong is what I'm after...to belong is the wish of every girl and boy."

Annie, Aaron and Dennis joined her in the chorus. They locked hands and pulled their dad, uncle, aunt, cousins and me into their circle. Mr. Smith's arms reached around each of them as we swayed to the words the children sang. Every eye brimmed with tears as smiles covered their faces.

They believed. And now they were a family. They belonged. Their dad had come back for them.

"Thank you for taking care of them and giving them time together when I couldn't," said Mr. Smith as I gathered my things.

"Now, I know why we did. I believed them," I said. "Welcome home." I waved as I walked out the door, feeling chills and cheers through my whole body.

Parent or Sister?

As the oldest, it was obvious Justine took the role very seriously. She was just 13 the first time she came to Camp To Belong Summer Camp. More than a year prior, Justine and her five siblings had been divided among five homes after the social service system determined their mother was unfit to care for them. They could not locate a home to take in all five siblings. While Justine and her sister Nicole, 10, were moved into the same home, their other sister and brothers were placed separately. They saw each other sporadically.

Justine clearly felt a tremendous void in her life. Each day and night had revolved around her siblings and her innate responsibility to take care of them when their mother couldn't or wouldn't. Now she wasn't there for them. Justine felt hurt about the possibility that her youngest brother could be forming stronger relationships with his foster family than his own relatives. She missed him and their special bond. She was afraid that when they saw each other again, he would think she was a stranger and not a sister. She worried that he was mad at her because she wasn't there for him like she'd always been in the past.

At least she had Nicole nearby and felt confident and needed as she looked out for her. Justine embraced the comfort in the parenting role.

While their other siblings were too young to attend Camp, Justine and Nicole looked forward to "sisterly" fun together.

From the moment they arrived, Justine's role was apparent. She helped her sister get ready each morning by picking out her clothes and fixing her hair. She helped Nicole at meals, making sure her eyes weren't bigger than her stomach and her plate was full of healthy food and not just sweets. She told her to be quiet when counselors were giving directions. She volunteered both of them to try an event first. She listened to the conversations Nicole had with other campers and corrected her wording if she didn't tell the story just right. While Nicole followed Justine's lead for the most part, bickering ensued from time to time. Justine would walk away in a fit of frustration until she could calm down and confront Nicole again. The pressure of parenting was becoming obvious by Justine's inability to focus on herself without constantly overseeing her sister.

"This week, you don't have to be a parent," I whispered in her ear. Justine's shoulders immediately relaxed. "You get to be a camper," I added. "We'll take care of your sister. You take care of you and focus on spending time with her." Justine gave me a hug. Without saying it, she knew I understood her actions and she appreciated that I lightened her load.

Justine absorbed the joys of Camp from the beginning. Not only was she willing to participate, she wanted to learn everything about our Summer Camp.

"Why do I see unicorns everywhere?" she asked.

"The unicorn is our logo and it means that each of our campers is unique and special," I answered.

The next day she presented me with a Playdoh® unicorn adorned with a bright rainbow over its head. She drew pictures of a unicorn on stationery. She created a big unicorn on our suggestion bulletin board for all to see. "I want everyone to feel special and unique everywhere they look," she said.

The Signature Life Seminar program intrigued Justine the most. Created by my dear friend Wanda and enhanced by my sister Andi, campers 14 and older were treated to a tour of the a university. At the beginning of the session, the campers were asked who planned on attending college. To our surprise, not one camper raised a hand. After several hours of career surveys, computer matches, presentations by military organizations and visits by community service representatives, every camper, including Justine, had a post-foster care system plan in mind.

Justine brought the materials back to Nicole and spoke incessantly of all the opportunities awaiting them. They ranged from being a nurse to joining the Navy to working with AmeriCorps and Upward Bound. Nicole made it clear she wanted to be just like Justine and scoured through the materials, asking question after question.

"I'm scared to talk to strangers in the system about my life," Justine said. That acknowledgment led to many discussions. She began to accept that these strangers could be her greatest advocates, especially if she voiced her feelings, thoughts and hopes of her journey in and beyond the system.

A Camp To Belong highlight occurred when Judge Hardcastle, an exceptional family court Judge, took time to visit our campers. "Tell me what you like and don't like about the foster care system," he requested. He listened to their resilient "out of the mouth of babes" statements. The children shared matter-of-fact comments such as "everything is fine" to outright outbursts of "everything is horrible."

Then Justine stood up, looked at the faces around the room, and spoke directly to the Judge. As she spoke, she stood taller by the moment while Judge Hardcastle listened intently and committed to taking her thoughts into consideration. Justine spoke about her siblings and the frustrations of not seeing them. She shared her thoughts about the Foster Care Review Board, put in place by the judicial system to create an opportunity for everyone involved in a case to meet in one room at the same time. Some of those people present, like her social worker, were familiar. Many others were behind-the-scenes representatives of the state or the community who gave expert or objective opinions to the proceedings yet were strangers nonetheless.

While Justine said she appreciated knowing so many people cared about her, she honestly stated her apprehension of so many strangers knowing about *her*…yet she knew nothing about *them*. Judge Hardcastle humbly admitted, "I didn't think about it that way. Thank you." Justine led the way for others to speak honestly and the Judge to respond with words of validation. We gave our campers a voice and Judge Hardcastle demonstrated that people in authority do listen.

Justine and Nicole lived with a very special foster mom they referred to as Grammy. Even though they lived under the same roof, Grammy witnessed a disconnect between the sisters and believed our Camp would help develop their bond. She felt excited about the closeness the girls displayed when they returned home. "They are just so happy. They shared all their camp gifts and meaningful stories with me. Thank you so much," she told me over the phone.

It felt wonderful to receive a special thanks from a foster mother and affirm her trust in our intention to keep their connection solid and roles clear. I occasionally called Grammy, asking to visit the girls and take Justine for some special time alone together.

As our friendship developed, I saw so much of me in Justine. In the midst of challenge, she didn't cast blame. Like my days in foster care, she went with the flow, full of concern but also full of hope for peace in her individual and family life.

Grammy required the sisters to attend church each Sunday. Justine and Nicole loved their church family. The congregation embraced their members' children, whether biological or otherwise. Its leaders invited them to participate in all activities, no matter how temporary or permanent their place in the community. The girls sang in the choir and attended the youth group meetings. On occasion, Justine and Nicole's biological mother came to church and I applauded the relationship between their mother and Grammy with a tough acceptance of respecting the parent in charge. I also saw a love between the girls and their mom, even though Justine was no longer filling in for her.

"Lynn, I would really like it if you came to church with me one day," said Justine. I was honored that she wanted to share her spiritual life with me. I was the only Caucasian person in the church and I instantly became part of the family. I felt chills down my spine from their renditions of joyous religious songs. Blessings of hope and healing abounded and the powerful energy of love engulfed the room.

As Justine left the pew, I watched her walk to the front of the church. I assumed it was time for the choir to sing and eagerly waited to hear the melodies from Justine, Nicole and the other youngsters who gathered on stage.

Instead, Justine approached the microphone. "I want to introduce a very special guest," she said to the congregation. I looked around thinking I wouldn't know the special guest because I was new. "This special guest is the founder of Camp To Belong and has done so much for my sister and me."

I stood, pushing my shoulders back and blowing Justine a kiss, as all eyes turned toward me, from every angle of the church. I looked into their sincere faces and back up at Justine. She motioned me to join her at the microphone. I shook in awe as I approached her.

I hugged her tightly, proudly recounting her gracious introduction in my mind, yet petrified to address the congregation as she handed me the microphone. But my fears dissipated instantly as I glanced at Justine, Nicole and Grammy, and caught glimpses of the smiling faces of those sitting before me.

"Thank you for honoring me as a part of your family, just as Camp To Belong honors siblings like Justine and Nicole into ours." The words just came. They were natural. They were real. At that moment, I had a new family, too, and was reminded how Camp To Belong made such an impression for a young girl to want to share it, and me, with her religious family.

Several years later, during a visit to Las Vegas with Andi, we tracked down Justine. We were happy to learn that all the siblings were back home with their biological mother. Justine was the last to go home because her foster care support team felt her mother needed to gain responsibility for each child and ensure Justine didn't become the parent again. Justine said she had felt anxious, but patient. She couldn't wait to reunite with her siblings in a sister role.

When we visited the entire family, we received a warm welcome and thanks from their mother. As we watched the kids talk to each other in the background, we shared our gratitude with their mother for finding a way to bring her children back home.

"I grew up in foster care," she said, "so maybe that's why they had to go there, too." I had to bite my tongue because I knew that her reasoning was unreasonable. However, we still applauded her for bringing them home.

We lost touch for a while, but easily picked up where we left off once I heard Justine's voice on the other end of the phone. "I haven't stopped thinking of Camp To Belong," she said.

"Camp To Belong hasn't stopped thinking about you. How would you like to come back?" I asked.

While there was silence on the other end of the phone, I knew she was crying when the sniffles became audible. I told her about the new Counselor In Training program for former campers, knowing that she'd just graduated high school and qualified for the position. Justine introduced herself to the other counselors by writing:

> *My experience was one of the best I've ever had. Most places have their ups and downs, but for me, CTB only had ups. It was easy to relate to everyone there and all the counselors cared. CTB means a lot to me. It allowed me to realize that, even though I was in a foster home, I was special too. I could do things with my sibling that I had never done before, just like other kids. I want to come to camp because I love being there*

*and I feel I owe it to allow these campers to have the
experience I had when I was at camp. Love, Justine.*

As a counselor, Justine learned things behind-the-scenes
that make Camp function. "It gives you a sense of doing something good for someone else," she told the Camp To Belong
family. Realizing that the campers looked up to her as a role
model, Justine felt a need to demonstrate to each camper that
she was there because she cared about them. She showed quiet
enthusiasm and genuine emotion as she absorbed each moment with appreciation. She talked about being a parent to her
siblings and a sister at the same time. She talked about the
squabbles with Nicole and their tight bond of friendship and
sisterhood. The campers listened intently. Many of the older
children nodded their heads as they related to her comments.

Justine's experience showed genuine acceptance as the
campers realized they shared similar experiences and feelings.

They were brothers and sisters, first and foremost, in a
world where they didn't need to be parents just yet.

Brother for Brother Advocacy

Darryl, I'm coming to California to speak to the teens and would love for you to speak to them too," I said over the phone.

"Sure, but what should I say?" he asked.

"Let them know how sure you feel about yourself and let your heart speak for you," I replied.

The young men and women filed in to the community center and took a seat in the chairs that lined the multi-purpose room. Slowly, I walked down each aisle and shook each person's hand, meeting their eyes, realizing there was indeed a purpose for my presence. "Thank you for being here," I noted with each hello. They needed to feel welcome and trust that I wasn't just another speaker filling time, but one who could meet them where they were.

"The S in the SisBroHood stands for showing up, as you did today," I said as I clapped my hands in applause for them. Showing up physically was one thing. Something told me they brought their minds and hearts to this event, too, and I eagerly said I appreciated them giving me the benefit of the doubt.

An independent living group comprised of teens in foster care in central California invited me to speak about my journey in the system. I asked Darryl to join me, believing his connection to the other kids would show credibility and insight into our shared message of triumph. Darryl exuded confidence and I knew he could reinforce my goal to encourage youth to take control of their own destiny. A former youth in care standing alongside a current youth in care demonstrates the potential of a safe, secure and supportive transition.

"L is for the loyalty my foster parents show me. They love me unconditionally every day," Darryl exuberantly told the audience as he glanced at me standing at the side of the stage. I gave him a thumbs up and I marveled at his courage to share his definition of L O V E with his peers.

After the L for loyalty in L O V E, Darryl shared, "O is for the obedience we have to our foster parents, ourselves and God to listen and embrace that love."

"V is for the violence," he stated next.

I shook, concerned and wondered what violence had to do with love. He continued, "The violence is how we feel when we're afraid to accept and trust the love shown to us while we're in the system."

"E is for being emotionally scared," he stated next. "We feel scared. We finally opened our hearts to love and we don't want it taken away."

He concluded, "L-O-V-E, when you give it a chance, will make you a better person."

His peers cheered and applauded. Youth speaking to youth was a precious gift.

Darryl had come to Camp To Belong Summer Camp with his younger brothers Ryan and Tom. Each of the boys lived in a different home. Darryl was not sure he wanted to be at Camp. He feared boredom, but knowing his brothers would be there ultimately convinced him to attend.

He displayed quiet poise, taking in his surroundings, constantly evaluating the ifs and whys of participating in camp activities. We encouraged him to take part for the sake of his brothers.

Brotherhood shined from the moment they took the trail to the dining hall each morning through the horse pasture to their walk up the trail each evening. Darryl hesitated to participate with the entire group, but we could count on his giving attention to Ryan and Tom.

He made sure they were harnessed in tightly at the climbing wall; he let them pick their places in the raft and fell in behind them on the riding trail. There to help *them*, he didn't realize how much he was helping himself.

Ryan had a sheepish smile. He knew how much Darryl cared for him and took his every word seriously. When Ryan gave Darryl a high five or pat on the back, they shared affectionate grins. When Darryl presented Ryan with his sibling pillow, he grabbed his brother in a tight hug. Tom took it all in, following in the footsteps of his brothers, doing what they did in a chorus of laughter.

Finally, on the last, bittersweet night of Camp, the counselors looked forward to sharing the triumph of brothers and sisters celebrating a week of the sibling bond. We also dreaded it as the reality of pending separation set in.

Darryl, Ryan and Tom ambled side-by-side toward the campfire. They proudly wore T-shirts created by Darryl, customized with "Brother" on the front of each. The setting sun was drizzling its pinks and blues over the Rockies, melding mountain silhouettes with those of the many brothers and sisters, their spirits and souls intertwined on this journey.

At the blazing fire, footsteps slowed and hearts beat faster as an unplanned friendship circle surrounded the dancing flames. The wood crackled and the blue and orange colors streaked the air with the wonderment of all gathered for our closing ceremony.

Chatter dissipated as each person peered into, and around, the fire, acknowledging its magnificent presence. Thoughts, hopes, fears and dreams came into focus.

Darryl, Ryan and Tom moved toward a log and sat together. They looked to each other for reassurance that the smells of nature and shadows of the trees would comfort their emotions. They listened as we set forth to speak of the significance of the sibling bond and the love we'd shared all week.

I watched Darryl glare at the flames of the fire, which drew his eyes skyward. Suddenly, his body crumbled and his shoulders caved in. One of our counselors went to his side and put her hands on his shoulders.

He sobbed, "I found myself looking for something I wasn't even sure I wanted anymore. But then God opened my heart and I saw that even if I didn't care for anybody, everyone still cared for me. You don't have to be with someone every day for them to love you. My brothers needed me as much as I needed them."

Camp To Belong obliterated the wall that had guarded his true emotion. He indulged his feelings and let loose at the campfire. At that moment, Darryl decided to rebuild his relationships with Ryan and Tom.

Upon his return from Camp, Darryl told his foster parents about his realization at the campfire. They excitedly joined him in planning to bring Ryan under their roof to celebrate a sibling family.

It was only a matter of time before the authorities heard their plea and honored it. Ryan moved from his foster home into the same foster home as Darryl. Together, they forged a bond that would also include ~~also~~ Tom, despite his living in another state with his paternal grandparents.

I asked Darryl to describe what happened that night at the campfire. He wrote:

> *My moment of truth came at the campfire. But my heart began to get prepared the moment I arrived at Camp To Belong. At the end of the campfire, I was changed by God's power to love not just myself but other people. After the campfire happened, it burned a place in my heart. I will never forget that night. That was the night that changed my life forever. I belong. Now I can look back at my life and myself, and see somebody totally different. Because of the love I found that night around the campfire, I can go and make a difference in this world.*

State Lines Converge

They lived on opposite sides of the state lines, two in Wisconsin and two in Illinois. Two lived in a foster home and two lived in kinship care. Yet, their hearts were in similar places.

Two brothers Dustin and Chris and their two sisters Amber and Heidi were beautiful. Through eyes that mesmerized, they communicated with each other without speaking. Their mere closeness exuded an undeniable connection. They giggled at their private jokes, only to make everyone feel a part of them. They had moments of sibling rivalry and moments of pure bonding. They shared many family meetings as a part of the Camp To Belong Sibling Enhancement program. It offers opportunities to "agree to disagree" on their feelings of the past, and "agree to agree" on their relationships for the future.

"I miss my sisters when they are not with me," shared Dustin when speaking of their separation across state lines.

"It is nice to know somebody loves me," cried Chris, realizing the love among his brother and sisters is present even when they are apart.

"I just feel so great that you let me and my family share the magic when everyone comes together," beamed Heidi when celebrating a tightened bond among her sister and brothers, and connection with new friends.

When the children miss, when they love, and when they come together with honesty, they understand the challenges that permeate inside and out. The Summer Camp Inspiration Forum for natural self-discovery became real for them. Camp To Belong didn't have expectations for the campers to speak out and share their stories, let alone their emotions. Every counselor embraced them in an unconditional environment where they could be themselves in the safety of those who related, cared and responded genuinely. Within this haven, the campers and counselors learned their inner beauty and profound thoughts. They learned they sometimes don't feel so beautiful because their thoughts were marred with lack of confidence and purpose. At Camp, they found their beauty and their thoughts became ones of hope and reward. All the time, their actions brought benefits we could never have planned.

Amber wrote:

> *When I went to Camp To Belong summer camp for the first time five years ago, I thought I was wasting my time. What I didn't know was that from Camp To Belong I would get a whole new perspective of life and what I wanted out of it. When I first went into foster care in '98, I thought it was the most shameful thing, it was something that I couldn't even tell my closest friend. I was the only one in foster care in my small town.*
>
> *I didn't know what others would think of me if they knew my dark secret of being in foster care. I went on thinking foster care was bad until my foster mother Jen told me I could go to Camp To Belong with my brothers and sister. I remember going to camp and*

just seeing so many kids like me. They were all in foster care. It was a place where I no longer had to hide my secret; I didn't have to face the fear of rejection of being in foster care any longer.

When I first went into foster care and moved away from my siblings, I had forgotten what they were like. My siblings were doing their thing in life and I was doing mine. I had forgotten what an important thing siblings were. When I went back to Camp To Belong again, hearing everyone talk made me stop and think I do need my brothers and sisters. They are all I have left. Of course, going to camp made me scared to death because I had so much fear towards life. I was scared to death of getting close to my brothers again in fear they would be taken away from me again, but Camp To Belong gave me the week I needed to assure myself my brothers would never be taken away from me again. Just from a week of camp my life changed forever. Who I am today is because of Camp To Belong. Lynn and Andi gave me hope for a brighter future; I remember them telling me I could do anything that I wanted, no matter what anyone else said. They let me realize I didn't have to set limits on what I wanted out of life just because I was a youth in care.

I will never forget how Camp To Belong gave me the courage to open up and let others know about my past. My past was something that was eating at me every day of my life. CTB let me know I didn't need to let my past eat me alive because my past wasn't my fault. In a way Camp To Belong saved me, and I could never thank Lynn and Andi enough for what they have done. Lynn and Andi are the two greatest miracles in the world.

As individuals and as sisters and as brothers, these four precious souls opened their hearts to themselves, each other and the Camp To Belong family. Yet the door for closeness opened even further. Before Camp To Belong Summer Camp, one of the girls said about her brothers, "We try not to think that they live in another state and try instead to think they are just on a long trip. We have been away from our brothers for over a year, and sometimes we get very lonely without them."

Loneliness turned into belonging as their relationship expanded. After Camp, Amber and Heidi's foster mother Jen embraced the sibling relationships among the girls and their brothers. Chris emancipated and Jen welcomed Dustin to join his sisters in her home. The incredible trio continued to share their daily lives and kept in touch with Chris whenever they could.

"Every action should have more than one benefit," teaches my mentor Mary LoVerde, who is also a spokesperson for Camp To Belong. Our organization started as a vision to reunite brothers and sisters who lived in separate foster homes. Little did we know our actions would bring a multitude of life-changing benefits far beyond our strategizing, let alone our imaginations.

It wasn't long before Andi and I realized Summer Camp gave us quality time to celebrate our own sisterhood. We hadn't realized the impact of standing before our campers as siblings and role models. It helped them accept that their own relationships would thrive after their journey in care and become meaningful like ours. Amber, Heidi, Dustin and Chris shared the acceptance completely.

One of the most exciting benefits we didn't anticipate was summed up by Jen who said, "Being with other children in foster care wasn't one of your primary purposes, but it has become a big benefit for all the kids. CTB isn't just about a sibling's family; CTB has become a big family."

The sibling connections continue to triumph. Camp To Belong siblings have been open to telling their stories. The kids joined me as I received the Oprah Winfrey Use Your Life Award in 2000 on national television. They courageously shared their emotions with the audience.

In 2002, Heidi, Amber, Dustin and Jen joined my daughter Jamie and I in Philadelphia to be honored by L'eggs Hosiery. I was named their Woman Who Shapes Our World. It was a tremendous honor, one that I felt a strong need to share with our campers. Camp To Belong may create the environment to shape our world, but it takes our youth to be open to a new shape.

Our greatest gifts include the benefits when our foster parents write to each other or to Camp To Belong. Here's one of hundreds of letters we've received.

> *Dear Fellow Foster Parents,*
>
> *This is the fourth summer my girls will be going to CTB, along with their two older brothers. While CTB has given them the childhood memories of being together that were taken from them when they entered foster care (at ages 10, almost 11, 13 and 15), CTB has given me a much greater appreciation of the importance of siblings. While the kids treasure the fun they have together, I treasure helping to keep the four of them connected after camp. I've also enjoyed getting*

*to know more about their childhood through their broth-
ers' eyes and am better able to see the "roles" that each
child plays in the family.*

*At times, my girls get into arguments with each
other — usually over competition for their brothers' attention. At times they drive me crazy (I, however, never
drive them crazy!), and I want to step in to 'help' them
in not hurting each other's feelings. I want all four of
them to get along...But then I remind myself that
siblings are supposed to argue, get their feelings hurt,
and sort things out for themselves. So I try to step
back and let them resolve things on their own, and I
cut them a little slack after they're back from camp
since their emotions are running amok.*

*Thanks for sending your kid(s) to this camp,
Jennifer Lea Bronsdon
Foster mom (and social worker with a treatment foster
care agency)*

Amber, Dustin, Heidi and Chris have a special camaraderie with other veteran campers. They could see the big picture by honoring CTB with the first donation received by campers pooling together their own money.

These siblings may have lived across state lines, but no
boundaries got in the way of bringing them together.

Post Script:

Dustin has graduated high school and is enjoying his studies at college. Chris is out on his own. Heidi is a high school
exchange student in Germany. Amber continues to hold down
the fort with Jen. They are becoming a *real* family as Jen takes
steps to adopt the siblings.

Goals

C an William come to camp this summer?" asked Robert.

It was going to be his fourth visit to Camp To Belong Summer Camp with his younger sister Angela, and he was planning ahead. "Robert, you know this camp is for brothers and sisters. Who is William?" I asked, assuming he wanted to bring a friend along.

"William is my brother," he said in an obvious tone. Perhaps I was supposed to know that fact already.

"Your brother?" I reacted, startled. "I didn't know you had a brother. How come we didn't know about him?"

"I don't know," he answered matter-of-factly.

"Well, how old is he and where does he live?"

"He's a year older than me and he lives with me."

"Lives with you? Why didn't you ever tell us about him?"

"I thought Camp was just for Angela and me."

"Didn't William ever wonder why he was left out?"

"Sure, but we just thought he wasn't allowed to come with us."

I placed a call to their social worker. "I understand Robert and Angela have an older brother," I stated.

"Yes, in fact they have three other siblings as well," responded their social worker.

"Well, why haven't we spoken about them coming to Camp?"

"No real reason. Two are adopted and another lives with Robert and William."

"We don't want any of them to miss out. Can we have them come to Camp this summer?"

"Unfortunately, the two children who are adopted probably won't be able to come. Their younger brother has some disabilities that would make it hard for him to experience Camp. But, sure, William can come."

There was no guessing about recognizing Robert and Angela's brother. Handsome, lanky William got off the bus wearing a familiar Robert-Angela grin. "You must be William," I shook his hand in awe of his stature and happy we finally knew about him. "Sorry we didn't know about you before, but we're glad you are here."

"No problem, glad to be here," he said, then looked around pointing to the Rocky Mountain Range and shaking his head in disbelief.

There was no doubt he was surprised at our excited welcome and amused at the organized chaos around him - the younger kids running around in circles, the counselors gathering sibling groups and luggage, the singing of Shake Your Booty - all had him laughing in moments.

Robert introduced his big brother to all the campers and counselors with a look of pride on his face. Angela walked in between her bodyguards who were reveling in their brotherhood and shyly taking her hands in theirs.

Robert could have been jealous of the attention William was getting as the new brother on the block, but he wasn't. He could have acted as the know-it-all telling him what we were going to do and how he was going to do it. But he didn't. He could have gotten upset that William was spending more time with Angela than him, but he wouldn't. Robert was just glad his family grew with Camp To Belong.

Robert was a natural spokesperson. He grabbed the other campers' spirits and attention by displaying his talent for golf and telling how his passion to succeed was fueled by his experiences at Camp.

"Camp To Belong taught me how to set goals," he said at the beginning of his talk at our Inspiration Forum. As he bounced a golf ball on the tip of his club countless times, the crowd started cheering, "You go, Tiger!!"

"First I wanted to get on the high school golf team. I did. Then I wanted to play in a tournament. I did. Then I wanted to get a par 7. I did. Camp To Belong taught me how to set goals. My next one is to be on the PGA tour and then wear the green jacket. And I'm going to give all my sponsorship money to Camp To Belong."

A standing ovation ensued. Sure, we were happy about the potential sponsorship money. But we were happier about his encouragement to the other campers suggesting they set goals too.

Robert and William flanked their little sister who took a piggyback ride from one and then sat on the lap of the other. They left Angela behind for the Life Seminar, but told her all about the college campus when they returned.

Making small talk over meals, they laughed heartily when a singing William led a chorus of "Boom Chick a Boom" and tossed the silly song to Robert for the next version in a style for everyone to copy.

Campers and counselors asked Robert why he wanted to come to Camp each summer. He said, "I didn't know there were so many other kids in foster care. I feel like I belong."

"What do you want to bring home with you?" one counselor asked.

"My sister in my heart," he answered without hesitation.

Sitting between her brothers, Angela glowed. She didn't say much, but she didn't have to. Her joy was evident in her comfort with her brothers. Then someone asked William what he thought about being at Camp. He wrapped his arms around Angela and said, "I love this girl."

The sibling pillow presentation took the breath out of everyone. "Angela, have I told you how much I love you? When you get out of care, I will take you wherever you want to go. I love you, Angela," wrote William.

Robert paved the way for the Counselor In Training program, saying he wanted to offer his insight and experience to other youth in the foster care system.

Standing at the climbing mountain, he urged other campers to take their time because he knew they could reach the top. He also urged them to feel the exhilaration of standing on the summit and celebrating the freedom of rappelling down.

Robert said, "Camp To Belong taught me leadership and how to accomplish my dreams." As a camper, he knew he was there to be with his siblings and participate in activities. As a Counselor In Training, he felt more responsibility to make sure campers had fun, went to activities and spent quality time with their siblings. "I have a second family here and now it includes William, too," he said. "This is another one of the goals I had in mind."

Big Daddy

A gentle giant slowly emerged into the lively registration room, decorated with balloons, with a smile as huge as his stature. Patrick was a well-known and respected social worker for the county. His robust personality and God-given belief in the potential of kids in care aroused a contagious stream of hope. We had invited Patrick to be a counselor not only to embrace the children, but also to rally the other counselors who needed a boost of confidence. Although he couldn't commit the time, he came to Camp To Belong Summer Camp to introduce himself as an independent living specialist. He chuckled as he wished us luck and had a twinkle in his eye. We knew he'd be back.

Several years later, Patrick came off the plane adorned with backpacks, pillows and snacks he'd gathered from the seventeen children he'd chaperoned from Las Vegas to our Summer Camp. A pied piper of sorts, all he had to do was look at the children and they ran to his side. They followed his lead to the bus that would take all of us to our reunion destination. Camp hadn't even started and he was already dragging his feet, with sweat rolling down his forehead. But, that bigger-than-life grin assured us all was right in his world.

In the back of the bus, he sat amid the children chattering non-stop about their first plane ride and the excitement (or hesitation) of spending a week away from home with their brothers and sisters. Patrick himself wasn't talking to anyone. He had his headphones on.

My immediate thought was, *Oh boy, we can't have headphones. We need to be available to the children at all times. The children aren't allowed to have headphones. We can't break our own rules.* But I believed Patrick had reason to zone out for a moment. After all, he had just spent two hours on a plane with 17 children. We were lucky he didn't stay on the plane and go back. We respected his space and extended him the benefit of the doubt.

Once we got to the campsite, I knew we didn't have to worry about breaking rules anymore. Our Olympic games were running full steam. Campers and counselors alike were doing barrel races, playing tornado, donning potato sacks and hoola hooping like they were with their best friends, not 150 strangers.

It was time for the bat race. Each individual had to run up to a bat, put his or her forehead on the handle, spin around six times and run across the field to tag the person on the other side. Getting dizzy wasn't my favorite way of having fun, so I took the opportunity to observe this "race for the gold."

There was Patrick, spinning around the bat, staggering, falling and then rolling all over the ground, crawling toward the next person. Everyone laughed loudly and furiously, even Patrick.

Every camper and counselor respected this kind man. His size brought a "yes, sir" kind of attitude. His tears brought a "he's just like me" understanding. We invited Patrick to be our Summer Camp Director in ensuing years and celebrated a master of leadership among us. He talked and everyone listened. He had lessons everyone wanted to hear.

Patrick sang silly camp songs and everyone sang along. Everyone wanted to share. He directed the kids with firmness and enthusiasm and everyone followed. He stood between Andi and I, and we felt like princesses among our bodyguard, knowing our labor of love was as solid as the man who stood for our vision.

Out of the quiet at the closing campfire with only the crackling of the fire to be heard came his roaring voice of song: "I believe the children are our future." Everyone shivered and adjusted to this priceless moment. Out into the starry mountain sky, as tears ran down Patrick's face, the eyes of campers and counselors alike brimmed with tears. They embraced the person next to them, looked toward the sky, toward Patrick, toward each other and cried together. We felt as one, filled with love and immense hope to continue that feeling of belonging and purpose. Indeed, these campers are our future.

Patrick is now our Big Daddy, named by our campers and counselors with love. In addition to his support of Camp To Belong, Patrick is a social worker, foster parent, adoptive parent, founder of a charter school and minister who has touched the lives of many over the years.

Patrick wrote:

> *I have been thinking about how I could thank you for the wonderful time that I had at camp. This was one of the best camps that I have ever attended, due to my personal family being able to share it with me. The method to the madness was second to none.*
>
> *If I had only one wish, I'd wish that every social worker could experience the love, power, and personal relationship that a camp, which reunites youth*

in foster care with their siblings, should model itself after.

I opened up my heart as well as my mind, and allowed myself to grow as a professional as well as a child. As a child, I allowed myself to be free to experience the pleasures of campfires, white water rafting, making sibling pillows and bracelets, swimming, horseback riding, and yes, even singing the silly camp songs.

As a professional, I opened my mind to the injustice and the pain that most states, counties and government officials have contributed to the youth in foster care, whom they vow to support.

This injustice begins with every city, county and state. There is a cry that should echo in every foster parent, adoptive parent, legal guardian, as well as grandparents, group home providers, etc. They, as well as their agencies, need to obtain knowledge about the fact that how they secure specified licenses in their homes (boys only, girls only, boys 0-8, girls 10-14) separates families.

In most cases, this process harms the youth emotionally, physically, and mentally.

It also damages their ongoing need to belong and to feel loved as a family. We, in a system trying to protect and support the abused and neglected, have also abused and neglected. I may stand alone in my thoughts, but in my heart, the children of our system stand strong.

I alone cannot change the minds of a nation, but if we stand together and fight together, we as a people can change the internal thinking as well as the systemic outcome of a nation of hurting and emotion-

ally withdrawn children. Now that I have released my pressures and frustration with the system and its fuzzy logic, I would like to sincerely thank you for the educational as well as the emotional experience that Camp To Belong has instilled in me.

This was an experience that I feel every foster parent, relative resource, social worker, supervisor, District Office Manager, elected official, guardian, and group home provider needs to experience. This experience has empowered me to dig deeper within my own self and to regroup my decisions. I have made a decision to make a life-saving change in the life of a family, and I will continue to press toward the mark of a kinder, gentler nation. This nation should believe that when it comes to sibling separation - although every case is different and every client or child cannot be saved - it is an important life-impacting decision to be made.

I feel that just knowing how heart-wrenching it is to be separated from the person or people you love can we, "the system," avoid inflicting pain on foster children. Then, and I mean only then, can we expect change to happen in the life of a child/family.

I truly thank Lynn and Andi and all the counselors and financial supporters who have stepped up to the plate and hit home runs in the life of a child and a family. I also challenge you, whomever you are, to help in the fight to save a hurting child, reach within your heart and become a voice within your community. Make this a priority in your life and take the time to discipline/train/teach our placement resources, our legal system, and our loving parents all over the world on the pain that is being overlooked at this moment, in reference to sibling separation. I believe that we should expect, as well as accept, the positive change in the lives of our children. Until this great day comes to pass, there will always be pain within the hearts of those who experience the personal trauma of sibling separations.

P.S. Thanks for the memories…
Patrick Harden

Priceless Blessings

"Volunteers aren't paid not because they aren't worth it, but because they are priceless." Unknown Author

Priceless is an understatement. Blessings can hardly describe our Camp To Belong Summer Camp volunteer counselors. They are individual, priceless blessings who come into our lives as strangers one moment and become family the next. They reach out to us with their unique interest in Camp To Belong and we reach back to invite them to participate in our labor of love.

While they know they will honor the campers with their unselfish and enthusiastic intention to touch their hearts, they don't realize how filled their hearts will be with memories they will cherish forever. Unselfish, caring, wise and vulnerable, they put "benefit of the doubt" into high gear. They often arrive "firm" and transition to "flexible." They jump into the trenches but are willing to stand on the outer rims, too. They listen and they hear. They accept without judgment and never gawk in disbelief. They feel with every part of their souls. They find a new part of themselves.

To be a counselor, it requires nine days away from home, family, business and friends. It means taking vacation time, sometimes paid time off and sometimes personal, unpaid time.

It means opening up their wallets to pay their way to our Camp destinations. It often means changing planes once, twice and three times, praying for smooth transitions between airport hubs and dragging a sleeping bag because it's hard to stuff in a suitcase. It means sharing every moment in close living quarters with other adults and kids whom they don't know. It means supervising youth they've never met before. It means eating camp food and guzzling powdered fruit drinks. It means smiling when they don't mean it and acting when they don't want to act. It means being "on" 24 hours a day. They live it. Sleep it. Dream it.

Our priceless blessings of counselors create a mosaic of people, some previously touched by out-of-home care and others with no ties to the system. Some want to give back to where they came from. Others want to honor the siblings they can't imagine life without. They all want to make a difference in the lives of their campers, not realizing the impact it will make on their own lives.

Within two days of training before the campers arrive, the volunteer counselors grow to become a cohesive family focused on the same goal - making the week one of the best of the campers' lives. They are former youth in care, children of adoption, foster parents, adoptive parents, social workers and CASAs. They are dance instructors, schoolteachers, college students, corporate executives, construction workers, nurses, data base administrators and Marines.

They enthusiastically greet excited campers as they come off an airplane or jump off a bus. They approach shy, hesitant campers with a soft smile and kind word. They sleep in cabins with cabinmates snoring and tossing and turning in the beds, sometimes dealing with a sleepwalker among them.

They hike up and down the long, long trails to the cabins to retrieve forgotten jackets, water bottles and chapstick. They sing "Singing in the Rain" and "Boom Chick A Boom." They referee small sibling squabbles and revel in the moment when the same siblings give each other a high five or a hug. They celebrate the first horseback ride or climb up the mountain. They make incredible connections with the campers and fellow counselors. They get pats on the back from their new friends and give themselves applause for stepping outside their box. They may not get along with each person, but they play alongside everyone. They laugh out loud. They cry in silence. They're disappointed when the campers don't trust their intentions, but they're happy when a light of connection turns from flicker to flame.

And just when they think they are ready to go home and sleep in their own beds, they realize they don't want it to end. It's over in a moment, but they want it to last forever.

The volunteer counselors of Camp To Belong are everyday people who experience the exhaustion of being hit by a truck one moment and enjoy the exhilaration of getting through to a camper who has a chip on his shoulder the next. They understand gratitude doesn't come easily from the campers, if it comes at all. They realize they may never know how much they affected a child's life. They come back for more.

Our counselors become CASAs, social workers, foster parents and adoptive parents. They look at their families differently and call their own brothers and sisters the moment they get home. Our volunteer counselors currently working within the system encourage new practices as they relate to siblings. Some alter their careers in order to participate in that change.

Jen Reed writes:

Imagine me... a 30-something executive in the cable television industry...meeting Lynn Price for the first time at a leadership program we were selected to attend. At that time in my life (and in my career), I looked at most people in situations like that from a "what can they do for me?" perspective. Basically, could she help me move forward? Boy, would she...but not in any way I could have ever imagined.

At one of our first meetings, Lynn shared with us (a group of 25 senior level women) the history of Camp To Belong and her commitment to sibling re-unification. I was enthralled by her passion and the fact that she was truly making a difference. Soon after, I sent in a donation check, thinking that was what folks like me did.

But it felt empty...like it wasn't enough. So I volunteered to be a counselor and headed to Colorado. For a week, I shed my business suits, e-mail and cell phone to jump into the open arms of Camp To Belong.

To say this week at camp changed my life is an understatement. Both the kids and counselors inspired me. Many of the counselors are social workers deeply committed to Camp To Belong's vision.

I left camp that week filled with love, a sense of accomplishment and, more importantly, the feeling that I had made a difference in a few young lives. I spent the plane ride home trying to decide how to hold on to that feeling forever.

It took some time, but one year later, I quit my job of ten years (a job I truly liked), entered the University of Pennsylvania in pursuit of a master's degree in psychological services and became a volunteer CASA (court appointed special advocate). Now, one year after starting graduate school, I hold that very master's degree and also a full-time position as a therapist for troubled teenage girls.

Some folks have called me courageous for making such a dramatic career change. I think of it a bit more spiritually. I met Lynn Price and stumbled upon Camp To Belong for a reason. Other things had shadowed the path I was meant to travel. Lynn and the wonderful kids at Camp To Belong helped me uncover the path that had been intended for me all along.

And, yes, I find that I now often recapture that wonderful feeling first uncovered at Camp To Belong in my daily work.

— Jen Reed, volunteer counselor, Camp To Belong, Colorado 2001

Every volunteer counselor has a place in my heart. They have honored me, Andi, the campers and other volunteers of Camp To Belong with their character, integrity, respect and sense of purpose.

They all have different reasons for coming to Camp To Belong Summer Camp. It's one thing to have a vision; it's another for others to heed the calling. I call them priceless blessings. Thank you may be only two words to say, but they speak of infinite gratitude.

We all belong.

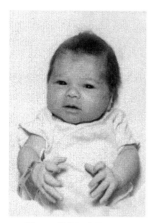

"Lynn," Birth Picture

Placed in the System with These Belongings

```
November 1, 1955      Jackie Lynn

   1 Rubber Pad
   2 Blankets
   4 Sheets
   5 Pajamas
   1 Yellow Robe
   7 pr Socks
   3 Bibs
   1 Carriage Hook
   2 Sweaters -yellow & rose
  10 Overhalls
  11 Tee Shirts
   8 Undershirts
   3 Kimonos
   3 Dresses                    Lamb
   2 Rec. blankets
     Rubber pants
   1 Pr. Shoes
```

Case Study Excerpt

JEWISH CHILDREN'S BUREAU

Name JACKIE LYNN PAUL A.K.A. Lynn Schreiber Parents   Sheet ___-3-___

PSYCHO-SOCIAL DIAGNOSIS:

At the time of referral, Lynn, 8 months old, was described as a healthy, attractive, and appealing infant.

Me and Queenie

Initially
Bernyce agreed that visits with the girls would not be
helpful to them until such a time as she was ready to
begin planning for their return to her home. While she
remained interested in her daughters, Bernyce did not
insist upon visits until 1962 when she was asked by the
State to begin contributing towards the girls' support.
At this time Bernyce became more insistant about seeing
the girls and began making plans for their return to her.
She planned to obtain a larger apartment, to support the
girls by working full time, and to have her mother live
with her to care for the girls when she was at work.
Attempts by the agency to help Bernyce understand that
her daughters, who had been in placement for six years,
might not be ready to leave their foster homes to live
with her failed. It was very difficult for Bernyce to
see that her daughters had made attachments to their
foster families and in reality had little memory or
attachment to her. It was felt that this would be
especially true for Lynn who had been placed as an
infant. Beginning in 1963 visits were arranged on
a monthly basis. This created considerable stress
and anxiety on both Lynn and her sister Andre.
Although Lynn was curious about seeing her mother and
her sister, she was also very fearful of her mother's
plans.

Case Study Excerpt

Me, the Big Sister, and Jeff

Dad, Jeff, Mom and Me

Case Study Excerpt

Mother and Me in the stark room at the Bureau

Jewish Children's Bureau Visit

Andi and Me at a Real Family Occasion

Andi, our Mother and Bucky Beaver at a Real Family Occasion

My Bat Mitzvah
Me, Jeff, Mom, Dad

Andi, our Mother, Me

Sisters

The Booth at the Restaurant

The agency felt that Lynn had made a very adequate
adjustment to school and that she could depend upon the
continued support and interest of her foster family.
The closing of this case was discussed and agreed to
by Lynn, the foster family, and the agency. This case
was closed on 8/1/74.

Case Study Excerpt

> Lynn, who reacted quite negatively to any discussion of her position as a foster child in the Schreiber home, refused to use her name, Paul at school. She wanted to be known in school as Lynn Schreiber

Case Study Excerpt

What's My Name?

CC-CH-D-Form 39   DECREE FOR CHANGE OF NAME (SINGLE FORM)

IN THE CIRCUIT COURT OF COOK COUNTY, ILLINOIS
COUNTY DEPARTMENT, CHANCERY - DIVORCE DIVISION

THE PETITION OF

JACKIE LYNN PAUL

78CH 417

No.

For change of Name

JUDGMENT

This cause having come on to be heard upon the petition filed herein and upon motion of petitioner's attorney, and the Court having read the said petition, together with the affidavit appended thereto, and the certificate of publication filed herein, and it appearing that previous notice of the intended application for a change of name was given by publishing a notice thereof in CHICAGO

DAILY LAW BULLETIN a newspaper of general circulation published in the County wherein the said petitioner resides, said publication having been made for three

consecutive weeks, the first insertion of which was at least six weeks prior to ....

JAN. 23 ...., 19 78, the said notice being signed by the said petitioner and setting forth the return day of this Court at which the said petition was to be filed, together with the name sought to be assumed, and the Court, being fully advised in the premises, doth find:

That all the material facts alleged in said petition are true; that the said petitioner is a resident of the State of Illinois and has resided therein continuously for a period of at least six months next

preceding .... JAN. 23 .... 19 78.
that the conditions mentioned and specified in an Act of the General Assembly of the State of Illinois, entitled "An Act to Revise the Law in Relation to Names," approved February 25, 1874, and in force July 1, 1874, and as amended, have been complied with; that this Court has jurisdiction of the persons and of the subject matter hereof; and that no reason appears why the prayer in said petition contained should not be granted.

It is therefore ordered, adjudged and decreed that the said petitioner's name be, and the same is

hereby changed from .. JACKIE LYNN PAUL ....
.... to .... LYNN SCHREIBER ....
by which said last-mentioned name shall be hereafter known and called.

After the Name Change, My Original/Revised Birth Certificate

SOME FAVORITE SPECIAL MEMORIES

Darlene and Me,
College Graduation

Audee and Me, Our 30th
High School Reunion

Lane and Me,
Planning our First
Card House

Barb and Me, My 40th
Birthday

Daddy's Little Girl, Dancing
at Darlene's Wedding

Chuck and Me, When We First Met

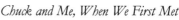

Lynn,

You know how much your father loved you. I understand you think he would accept your marriage. As you know he never did anything on the spur of the minute. I am sending you a copy of his will that has to do with you.

SECOND CODICIL
TO THE WILL OF
ALEX SCHREIBER

DRAFT

I, ALEX SCHREIBER, of Skokie, Illinois, hereby make this second codicil to my will dated February 28, 1968.

FIRST: ~~████████████████~~
~~████████████████████████~~

SECOND: I hereby further amend my said will by deleting the FOURTH ARTICLE in its entirety and substituting the following FOURTH ARTICLE therefor:

FOURTH ARTICLE

I give the residue of my estate, excluding any property over which I have power of appointment, to my wife, if she is living on the thirtieth day following the day of my death. If my wife is not then living, I give said residue of my estate as follows: ~~████████~~

2. I give the sum of ~~████████~~ our mutually acknowledged child, LYNN SCHREIBER (also sometimes known as Jackie Lynn Paul), if she survives me and if she be either unmarried or married to a man of the Jewish faith who was born of parents who were both also born of (not converted to) the Jewish faith. If neither of the preceding conditions are met, I give her the sum of ONE DOLLAR ($1.00).

Our Wedding

CAMPER STORIES

Darryl

Bryan

Randy

Big Daddy

Camp photos are limited due to confidentiality.

STILL PINCHING MYSELF

Oprah's Angel Network
presents

The USE YOUR LIFE Award

to

Lynn Price
Camp To Belong

Thank you for Using Your Life
to be a loving force in the world.

Oprah Celebration With
Lifetime Friends, l to r,
Nancy, Darlene, Shelley,
Andi, Me, Lane

My Proudest Legacy

Tanner, Addison, Jamie

Sibling Rivalry

Sibling Connection

*At Camp To Belong
Summer Camp*

*Andi and My
Immediate Real
Families,
l to r back,
Chuck, Me,
Andi, Ed, Bob
l to r front, Dan,
Addison, Jamie,
Tanner, Matt*

My Families

Larissa, Jamie, Tanner, Addison

Jennifer and Zach's Wedding, l to r back, Addison, Zach, Jennifer, Me, Chuck l to r front, Tanner, Jamie

My Real Immediate Family

SISTERS

*First Annual Camp To
Belong Summer Camp*

Venice Beach

Camp Clowning Around

*Camp To Belong Sibling
Pillow*

Part Three

The Power and Passion of Real Belonging

To Belong

THE CAMP TO BELONG THEME SONG

TO BELONG TO A LOVING FAMILY,
WHO'S PROUD FOR ME TO BE JUST ME,
ENVELOPING ME WITH FRIENDSHIP,
MAKING MY HEART AND SOUL COMPLETE.

TO HAVE SOMEONE TO TALK TO,
TO KNOW THAT SOMEONE CARES,
WHEN I NEED SOMEONE TO HEAR ME,
IT'S NICE TO KNOW THAT SOMEONE'S THERE.

CHORUS:TO BE ME, FULL OF LAUGHTER,
TO BE ME, FULL OF JOY,
TO BELONG, IS WHAT I'M AFTER,
TO BELONG, THE WISH FOR EVERY GIRL AND BOY.

Written by Lynn Price and Terry Prince, Performed by Terry Prince and campers, 1995

Daughter and Sister by Choice

 My parents are going to put me in foster care," said Jenny in an everyday conversational tone.

My checkbook fell to the floor and my eyes focused on her. "Excuse me, did you just say your parents are putting you in foster care?" I asked, shaking my head from side to side.

Jenny was our thirteen-year-old baby-sitter. I was writing her a check and still had my coat on so I could drive her home.

I always knew she was wise beyond her years. She was our favorite baby-sitter; her role of sitting was more of caring, of teaching our kids and of sharing our family life. At such a young age, she was strikingly beautiful, already over five feet tall with long blond hair and cat-like eyes. Everyone would turn toward her as she walked into a room, yet she never indicated that she knew she was, let alone wanted to be, the center of attention. Chuck and I trusted her implicitly with our children. Her self-confidence stood solid.

We had no reason to think she had any challenges at home.

"Foster care is not an option," I said, hugging her tight.

I removed my coat and motioned her over to the couch. We spoke for several hours about the challenges she faced at home and her parents' inability to care for her at that point in time. They felt her best option was foster care, so she would be taken care of while they evaluated their circumstances. I suggested a different plan.

"Mrs. Howard, I'd like Jenny to live with our family for a while," I said to her mom after getting Jenny's permission.

I didn't need to know why they couldn't or wouldn't want to take care of Jenny, their own daughter. I didn't need to know if Jenny had done or experienced something that brought this situation to fruition. I just knew she was already a part of our family and we would take care of her.

Jenny moved in and automatically became the big sister in our family. Although Addison, Tanner and Jamie were still very young and may not have totally understood, they welcomed her into our home. Jenny didn't have any brothers or sisters and the mutual love shared with my children felt like a natural sibling connection. While she continued her role as babysitter, our kids treated her as their big sister. Chuck and I treated her as our daughter.

After discussing educational needs with Jenny's parents, I took her to register at the nearby Catholic high school. I made sure she had uniforms and school supplies and sat with her many evenings helping her with her homework. Chuck taught Jenny to drive. We were a family.

We supported her decision to return when her parents were ready for her to come home.

We celebrated her high school graduation and her journey to college.

While a series of connections and estrangement occurred between Jenny and her parents over the years, she came back to our unconditional acceptance whenever she needed to do so.

Jenny became our daughter and sister by choice.

I was honored when she handed me a flower, "for the mother of the bride," on her wedding day. Jamie beamed at being her flower girl and Addison and Tanner looked dapper in their tuxedos as they walked down the aisle.

"Hi, Grandma," Jenny said sweetly over the phone when she shared the news of their first child.

At Thanksgiving, Jenny and her husband Zach hosted a family dinner, which her mother and father attended. It was the first time I had seen them in years. Jenny and her mother had recently reconnected again after the baby was born and I was thrilled she celebrated the role of Grandmother as well.

Standing in the kitchen cleaning the dishes, her mother said to me, "I'm sorry…"

I put up my hand to suggest she pause and reached out to hug her. "No need to be sorry now. Look around us. We are one big happy family," I said.

Logan and Lexi call me "Grandma Price." Of course I have the most beautiful grandchildren in the world. Not only do we have a daughter and sister by choice, we are blessed with grandchildren by choice.

From Stranger to Mom

Maybe it was their sandy, blonde, cropped haircuts. Or their blazing blue eyes. Or the way they sat quietly by each other's side, gazing at the other campers around them. Or the furtive glances one snuck at the other when the other one wasn't looking.

At 11 and 9, Bryan and Josh came to the very first Camp To Belong Summer Camp. Their little sister Samantha was only four - too young to experience a sleep-away camp from her foster home and to understand the significance of the sibling bond we emphasized 24 hours a day. Their older sister Christina lived with an aunt. While she was open to spending time with her brothers, she wasn't available to attend Camp that year.

The boys lived at a group home. While Bryan and Josh were separated from Samantha and Christina, they were the only two available for Summer Camp.

Bryan's and Josh's connection was tested by their group home environment and the fact that one of the brothers made the 9-1-1 call when the other didn't want it to be made. Their being separated from their mother and their sisters was an excruciating burden that pushed them apart rather than pulled them together.

Bryan and Josh were quiet, gentle spirits who exuded gratitude through simple turned-up grins on their angel faces. They trustingly displayed their willingness to experience all opportunities for adventure offered. Their walls of separation crumbled as their chatter built trust between them. In essence, they forgot where they lived and why, so they could remember who they were.

The boys became each other's greatest cheerleaders during a softball game as they waved each other crazily around the bases. During a martial arts demonstration, they sparred innocently but wouldn't dare to strike each other down. They rolled their eyes as they made dream catchers for each other, yet they didn't hesitate to share their dreams. They rallied around a make-believe campfire and ate gooey s'mores while shyly singing silly camp songs. As brothers, they fully modeled a strong sibling bond.

Just by their mere presence, I felt sure of the reasons we did what we did at Camp To Belong Summer Camp. They were building a relationship for the future and by forming memories at Camp, we built hope for their future success. I wondered what their futures would look like and I knew I wanted to be a part of the unfolding.

Maybe it was somewhat selfish. It's hard to let go of *any* of the kids after Camp ends, but I just couldn't get these two young men out of my mind. So I called my CASA director Betsey, and shared my vehement interest in serving as a CASA for Bryan and Josh. I crossed my fingers that they didn't already have an active volunteer assigned to them. I ached to be a voice for those too skeptical to speak yet having so much to say. Betsey's desire to match CASAs with children they were sure to impact supported my reasoning. I felt a calling for these boys, and she was willing to take the call. I was thrilled she gave me the go-ahead to talk with them about an enhanced and on-going relationship.

Butterflies filled my stomach as I traveled to the group home to meet with Bryan and Josh, and to share the news. I hadn't asked them how they felt about my being their CASA ahead of time. I didn't want to disappoint them if there was a reason it couldn't happen. Now, I didn't want to be disappointed if they weren't interested in my new proposed role. *What if they really didn't care the way I did?* I worried.

We lingered in the courtyard. I motioned them to sit on a bench while I paced anxiously before them. I asked if they understood the responsibilities of a CASA. We discussed how this volunteer role would afford me the opportunity to serve as their voice as they journeyed through the system. They both replied that they understood because they met many of us at Camp.

"Well, how would you feel about my being your CASA?" I asked, casting my eyes on each of them.

"That would be cool," Bryan swiftly replied.

"Sure," followed Josh.

They nodded their heads enthusiastically.

I met sweet Samantha who was flourishing in her foster home with a family eager to adopt her should parental rights be terminated. Then I met Christina who was enjoying her life as part of a family and, while not thrilled with having a CASA, she was open to the possibilities of my bringing her together with her brothers and sister from time to time.

On several occasions, we all met for a visit to the park or an ice cream cone. It was clear the girls enjoyed stability;

my true challenge was to honor the boys in their home away from home.

I met their mom and supervised visits between her and any combination of her children. She clearly had feelings for them and a concern for their welfare. However, her case plan was lengthy and her ability to accommodate all its provisions lost stride with passing time.

Bryan and Josh came to our second annual Camp and stood as veteran campers for the new kids. They instinctively made sure that everyone felt welcome as they came through the lobby door of the University of Las Vegas dormitory.

When the firemen came and hosed down the kids in a laughter-filled water fight, the boys made sure everyone got a chance to hold the hose. When we scurried to be the first in line to ride the roller coaster at Circus Circus, they made sure those who wanted the front car got the right place in line. When special guests came to visit, they encouraged the campers to speak out about their concerns of being in foster care. They modeled brotherhood and maturity about their place in our family.

I vowed to do whatever it took to ensure these resilient boys wouldn't fall through the cracks of the system, and started to put a safeguard in place.

Time was running out for their mom to meet case plan demands; the possibility of terminating parental rights hung on the horizon. I knew the girls each had a family and would be fine. I also knew both of their families, while unable to take the boys, would continue to honor their sibling connection whatever the future held.

With the love and support of my family, we decided to take the required steps to become a foster family. I asked Bryan and Josh how they felt about yet another new role and the aspect of living with us. They were excited. My kids were already calling them brothers and celebrating their birthdays in our sunny kitchen or weekends on our boat at Lake Mead.

To pursue the foster care license, I had to give up my role as their CASA because it was a conflict of interest. That meant I had to relinquish their case and transitioned them into the CASA care of a trusted colleague. The transition felt right at first. But it took some shocking turns. I thought that intending to become their foster family would only bring us closer. Surprisingly, by the very act of having new roles and new rules, distance among us ensued.

Bryan and Josh first moved from the group home to a family foster home. I knew the foster parents who were aware of our history together and our intentions to take over foster care for the boys. I knew the caseworker and he knew our history with the boys as well. I knew the new CASA who was also familiar with our history and our intentions. My family wasn't just any family.

But over time the communication decreased. We went from knowing everything about daily life to not knowing a lot of anything in their lives. We went from seeing them often to seeing them at the sporadic discretion of the system. I worried that they thought our family interest was waning, that the sense of belonging I wanted to give them was being taken away. I respected the system for its rules and protocol requiring us to complete training and investigations to take place for licensing. However, the risk of disconnect increased. We forged ahead.

At that point, Chuck received a job transfer and we agreed to leave Las Vegas for Denver. I knew instantly, the move would affect the boys. I paced across the Mexican tile floors in the kitchen with the long phone cord twisted around my fingers as Mr. Connor, their caseworker, said, "You cannot foster out of state. The plan still calls for reunification with their mother and they cannot cross state lines."

I knew all my objections wouldn't do any good. That was a rule and a good safety net. I knew I couldn't be hypocritical if I fought to take the kids and further separate them from their sisters. I was all about sibling reunification, so how could I pursue the move? Because, I reasoned, I had a commitment to their connection and communication regardless of where they lived.

So we left Las Vegas, and we left Bryan and Josh behind. We couldn't even say good-bye.

Four years later, I received an e-mail gift of a lifetime. Their CASA asked if Bryan, Josh and Samantha could come to Camp. I was jolted by learning they were still in the system. The "what ifs" cascaded into my mind. *Just, what if, they had become my sons back then?*

"Of course, they can come to Camp," I wrote back. If their CASA had been able to see through the computer, she would have watched me jumping up and down as I replied to her with exhilaration.

I eagerly waited at the terminal gate to meet all of our Las Vegas campers, who'd come to Colorado for the first Camp in this state. Samantha didn't recognize me. To avoid any confusion, I just introduced myself and welcomed her. She had that same devilish grin I remembered. I soon learned that her foster/adopt placement didn't happen.

"Remember me?" I asked Josh.

"Sure," he responded, just as confident as the day I asked if I could be his CASA.

I looked around for Bryan, only for the chaperone to tell me he'd been in trouble back home. They would not allow him to come to Camp. My heart sank. Secretly, I became livid at the fact that missing Camp To Belong Summer Camp was used as a punishment.

"He got in trouble so he couldn't come to Camp with his brother and sister? Couldn't they come up with another consequence?" I tried to reason with the chaperone.

It was evident I shouldn't fight the fight and, while I missed seeing the boys as brothers, I celebrated having Josh and Samantha join the Camp To Belong family. They had a wonderful time and we made sure they made memories to bring home to Bryan. I decided it wasn't appropriate to bring up the past. As we hugged good-bye, I was thankful for my reunion with them.

The next summer, I stood in the parking lot after the Las Vegas bus arrived at the campsite. I knew Bryan, Josh and Samantha were supposed to be coming again, but I held onto my emotions to avoid another disappointment if any one of the three was a no-show.

"Hi, let me help you," said one young man as he picked up a camper's bags.

"Hi, I'm Lynn," I said offering a handshake.

"Lynn, I'm Bryan."

I reached up to put my hands on his shoulders. He'd grown up right before my eyes.

The last time I saw him, he was 12. Now he stood tall as a 16-year-old young man.

"I've never forgotten you," spilled out of my lips.

"Me neither," he said, as we hugged and laughed at the wonderful moment of reunion.

Then Josh came stumbling into the parking lot and we had a group hug. He was on crutches after injuring his knee, but he wasn't missing Camp. This time Samantha didn't come. A sudden illness had forced her to stay behind.

At Camp, even with a cast on his leg, Josh climbed up and rappelled down the mountain while Bryan stood, watching his brother's every move, cheering him up and down. They stood side by side at the climbing wall and scrambled toward the top at the sound of "go." Bryan wrapped plastic around Josh's foot as we ventured into rafts floating down the Colorado River.

They sat side by side at our Life Seminar and listened intently to details of career, military and community service options for the future. They made pillows for each other, and one to bring home to Samantha.

"I went to Camp To Belong back in Las Vegas in the beginning when it was at a school. I can't believe how much better it has gotten. This place in the Rocky Mountains is phenomenal. I'm always going to come back. When they let me, I'm going to be a counselor," boasted Bryan to his brother and newfound friends.

I had to know what the boys thought about our lapse in communication. Up until that time, I hadn't even broached the topic of my move from Las Vegas. I didn't know what they had been told about it. And I didn't know if they felt abandoned. Perhaps they harbored feelings of distrust because I told them I would always be there for them. Just maybe they missed me as much as I missed them.

My tears started flowing before the words came out of my mouth. "I just want you to know I never wanted to leave you."

"I know that," Bryan responded with tears filling his eyes.

"I couldn't take you with me and they wouldn't let me say good-bye. I have never stopped thinking about you."

At this point, Josh's eyes filled with tears, too, and Bryan's started flowing. "I have never forgotten you or what you have done for us. You have always been in my heart," said Bryan.

Nothing more needed to be said. The tears, silence and deep hugs spoke to the time lost and the words not said, and the trust had carried across the distance of time and location. The feeling of reward was tremendous.

The next summer, all three siblings came to Camp. It was joyous. They were real siblings, complete with sibling rivalry and sibling connection.

The facts that her new foster mom supported the re-union, that the CASA secured these siblings' attendance at Camp and that she expressed her love for her brothers brought a standing ovation.

When Bryan turned 18, he evaluated his options while keeping in mind his multiple moves from a boys' home to a shelter and a foster home to independent living. During a visit I made to Las Vegas, we discussed what his future would look like beyond graduation and the system. We talked about his road to college, career, marriage and becoming a father.

I asked him to think about whom he would share all those moments with as he delves into new friendships and loves in his life. I asked whom he would include from his past to cel-ebrate his future. I told him the story of Charlotte Lopez, the Miss Teen USA who was adopted at seventeen years old. When asked why she wanted to be adopted when she could be free and on her own, she spoke of her foster family, their participa-tion in her successes and her own family in the future. She also valued siblings. I told Bryan I would never take his mom's place, but I would be proud to be a part of the family he comes home to.

"It's never too late. I know deep down your mother loves you. But your future is ahead of you. You need a family to come home to. I offer mine."

I listened to his voice mail over and over again when I returned home. "I've been thinking about what you said," were the first words I heard. "I would like for you to be my mom." I doubt I've ever heard a greater compliment. I didn't know what that meant in semantics or reality, but I knew the feeling of saying and hearing it was an honor.

Bryan and Josh's photo adorns my desk. Samantha's poem hangs on my wall. "Much love" written on the back of a Disneyland postcard from Bryan stands under a magnet on my fridge. While his journey in the system and the potential of yet another role continues, I know these kids will be forever im-printed in my heart. Most important, I know wherever their journey takes them, they will have childhood sibling memories.

In another voice mail, Bryan said "Hi MMM, I just got a cell phone and wanted you to be one of the first to know." I left a voice mail back, "Did you say 'hi man' or 'hi mom?' If you said man, back at ya. If you said Mom, wow, what can I say?"

In a subsequent e-mail he wrote:

> *Dear Mom,*
>
> *I can't wait for camp. I walk (graduation) the 4th, 6 days before camp. I'm still not sure what time we walk but I have to keep this short because I'm kinda busy. I am still trying to get a job. And on top of that I have been working on making my rap CD.*

It's more like a demo, just a small CD, about 5 tracks and I will try to give it away to some major producers in the record industry. Hopefully I will get a chance and go somewhere with that. Everybody has high hopes for me and believes that I can do it. I have enough connections to get to places that will give me the chance to go somewhere, but we will see. Anyhow, love ya much. Thank you for keeping me in the loop hole and everything you have done.

your son,
Bryan

"Dear Mom" and "your son." How do I describe how I feel? There are no words.

"Josh said he is all for me being a part of your family," said Bryan. The fact that he discussed this relationship with his brother spoke volumes about their connection.

"He's whatever part of the family he wants to be, too," I responded.

It was such a testament to have Bryan present at our introduction of Camp To Belong Nevada to the Las Vegas community. There was not a dry eye in the house, including Bryan's, as he shared the memories of his days at Summer Camp with his brother and sister and the impact the experiences continue to have in his life eight years after his first camp.

After the event came to a close, Bryan presented me with a stuffed lion and a plaque. "I bought myself one of these lions, too," Bryan said. He had remembered how I loved lions and the fact they stand for courage.

The plaque read, "A Parents' Special Place. There's no way to repay all you've done for me. There's no word to express how much you mean to me. But there is a special place beyond word and deed lying deep within my heart that you own exclusively. It's a place that holds respect and all the love you're due. And I want to tell you now it's always there for you." He explained that it was written by Stravina.

Christina was providing guardianship for Josh. Samantha was in a foster adopt home. Bryan was in an independent living apartment. An adoption is about to take place. Bryan is no longer a stranger. At nineteen years old he will become my son and a sibling to my children.

Sweet Larissa

Let me see if I got this straight," I said to the Arapahoe County Intake Worker on the other end of the phone.

I wanted to understand the urgency in his voice and the scope of his reasoning for calling my family. We actually lived outside Arapahoe County and cases seldom crossed county lines. *There must be something or someone very special here,* I thought.

I reviewed my notes and summarized the facts. A four-year-old little girl's father received custody after a long court battle in Colorado. He traveled to Kentucky for a new start and got himself in hot water. The young girl was subsequently placed in a foster home in that state. She lived there for three weeks, the family fell in love with her and wanted to adopt her. But the system had to bring her back to Colorado where the case had been initiated. Terminating parental rights needed to be addressed in conjunction with the past and current case. In the interim, she was placed in a metro Denver shelter. The shelter takes kids for only 90 days and she had reached 88 on the day of the call. The intake worker wanted her to come to our home temporarily. A judge would determine if sending her back to Kentucky was the right thing to do.

"Is this what you call the best interest of a child?" I asked. "Does she have any brothers and sisters?"

"Larissa doesn't have any brothers or sisters, and we've been told you are just the type of person Larissa needs."

I thought placing her with us was certainly in her best interest. As much as I stewed about the place-to-place movement of the child, I knew protocol had its merits and perhaps my family could ease the burden of transition. I had walked in her shoes. My children, Jamie, Addison and Tanner would be happy to be her siblings.

Jamie had asked daily for a baby sister. Chuck and the boys knew the day would come when our family would expand again. While we all knew the placement would be temporary, we felt eager to welcome Larissa into our home.

As I led the way to the front door of the shelter, I took a deep breath. I stopped before knocking on the door so I could look into the eyes of each one of my family members to confirm they were still with me on this decision. They each gave me a positive nod.

We stepped through the front entrance and into a living area of the shelter that was actually like a home. The walls were brightly painted and toys adorned every nook and cranny of the room. The staff member welcomed us warmly and took us on a tour of the children's home away from home. Each room had its own personality. The belongings of the children were either neatly put away or displayed for their comfort and security.

From the corner of the family room, a little girl turned around and looked us up and down.

"Larissa, I'd like you to meet your new family," the staff person motioned her to come over.

Her eyes swept me off my feet right away. These huge brown medallions were filled with sadness, yet I could see the glimmer of hope deep inside them. She wasn't interested in meeting us at the moment. She turned around and continued to play with the puzzle she'd placed on the table beside her.

A few minutes later, Larissa passed in front of us and went into her room. In a matter of moments, she started bringing things out to show us. She let Jamie hold her little teddy bear. She held up some dressy shoes. She pointed to some pictures of other children in the shelter. Then she took my hand and walked me to the puzzle and started playing with the pieces. Chuck and the kids came over one by one. Each of us surrounded the table and helped her put the pieces together.

This was like her life. So many puzzle pieces, yet we were the family already connected to her by putting the pieces together.

"Would you like to bring your teddy bear and clothes to our house?" I asked.

"Can I bring the puzzle?" she asked back.

"How about if we go to the store and you pick out your very own puzzle?"

"Yes," she shouted, grinning from ear to ear.

It was time for our family to leave. We couldn't take Larissa home that day because the procedures dictated that we should say good-bye, let her adjust to the thought of leaving, then come and pick her up the next day.

During the ride home, each of my family members commented about the vibrancy of little Larissa. Jamie couldn't wait to tell everyone about her sister. The boys liked the idea of being big brothers. Chuck glowed at the fact that my wish to be a foster mother would finally come true. The whole family was already smitten. We went home and replaced Jamie's single canopy bed with a bunkbed. She was so excited that she would get to share her room with her new baby sister. The boys made "welcome home" signs. We were ready to welcome our new family member!

I decided to pick up Larissa on my own because I knew I had to establish the first relationship. As I walked through the shelter to the backyard in awe of the happy spirit exuding throughout, I felt refreshed at the prospect of having another daughter.

Larissa was swinging on the swingset. Her beautiful eyes caught mine and, in an instant, she flew off the swing, running into my arms.

"Hello Mommy. I'm ready to go," she boasted happily.

I couldn't believe it. She called me Mommy. Her immediate trust was more than I could ever imagine. While I thought my part was to give Larissa emotional support, she'd already boosted mine to the sky. Singing and grabbing her belongings, she ran to each of the kids in the courtyard and in the shelter. "I'm going to my new mommy," she told everyone.

I didn't have to tell her to get in the car seat we'd just purchased for her. She just took her place like she'd been in the seat, in my car, dozens of times before.

"Where's Daddy and my new big sister and brothers?"

She didn't take any time accounting for her new family. I told her they were at work and school, but would be excited to see her in the evening.

Our furry little puppy Romeo met her at the door, creating a scene from a Christmas photo. In seconds, they were rolling around on the floor and, as Romeo's tail wagged, Larissa giggled. I could have let her stay there all day.

"Larissa, are you hungry?" I asked. She started looking around our home like Cinderella looked at the prince's palace. "Let me show you your room," I prodded.

She jumped on the top bunk and pointed to all the pink hearts that shined on the wallpaper next to her bed. We brought her belongings to the room and she went up on her tiptoes to get hangers in the closet so she could put away her clothes. We put her teddy bear near her new pillow. Then she skipped out of the room on a treasure hunt to see the boys' rooms and basement playroom. We settled at the kitchen table and shared peanut butter and jelly sandwiches. She picked away the crust of the bread just like every other kid did.

"Larissa, you know, I was once in foster care just like you," I said.

"Where did your mommy and daddy go?" she asked.

"I'm not sure. But I want to take care of you just like my foster mommy and daddy took care of me."

She kept eating her sandwich and was eager to get back to Romeo. Nothing more needed to be said.

When we picked up the kids at school, it was like show and tell. Larissa and I got out of the car and each of my kids brought their friends over to meet their new sister. Larissa took each of my kid's hands and they responded with a hug.

Jamie, Larissa and I arrived at the Brownie meeting to a new round of welcomes. While Larissa started out sitting on my lap, a few moments later she was singing Brownie songs and sitting on Jamie's lap.

When Chuck came through the door that evening, Larissa ran to him, too.

"How was your day?" she asked.

"It's great because you are here," said Chuck, scooping her into his arms.

Larissa fell into our routine immediately. At bedtime, she put on her pajamas, brushed her teeth and laid out her clothes for the morning. Each of the boys came in to say good night and Jamie read her a story. She fell asleep so peacefully. I watched her sleeping wondering if her dreams were as positive as this day had been for her. Or did nightmares of her journey ever fill her head?

For the next five weeks, Larissa graced our family with a humor, softness and intelligence that taught us so much. She talked about her mom and dad from time to time as thoughts of them floated through her mind in innocent conversations.

She offered stories about the meals that her mom cooked or the hobbies her dad had. She spoke of them happily without judgment and with pure acceptance.

She mesmerized my children and knew how to make each feel special. When it would come time to get out of the car, she would say, "I am not getting out this time until Tanner unbuckles my seatbelt." I'll be darned if Tanner didn't go back to the car and undo her seatbelt.

"The only person who can read a book to me today is Jamie," stated Larissa. Jamie, with a huge smile, grabbed a book and off they would go.

And Addison would just look over at her from time to time and say, "How are you doing, Larissa?" She would shyly look over at him and say, "Great, Addison!"

Chuck, who worried about how wrapped up I'd get with Larissa, got wrapped up himself, especially when she ran into his arms after a day's work.

Larissa and I were buddies. It was just that plain and simple. With the comfort of being together each day, we had an unspoken bond of love and respect.

However, I knew the reality of temporary placement. She was going to be moving on to Kentucky at some point in the near future. But as much as I tried to keep an emotional distance, my emotions got the best of me.

Her former foster mother and future adoptive mother Pam called about once a week. Pam sincerely showed concern about Larissa and expressed thanks that she was in our care. I was thrilled about her love for Larissa and proudly honored my place in the transition. Her social worker was determined to move Larissa to Kentucky as soon as possible.

Larissa and I had this incredible understanding. We giggled together, laughed and played. She easily kept herself busy while I attended to other things. She frolicked with the kids the moment they walked through the door. They always stopped what they were doing to give her the attention she deserved.

Everyone in our world knew Larissa, from the carpool line at school to the people at Starbucks. After sending an e-mail to Chuck's business colleagues announcing our new arrival, Larissa received nine boxes of clothes, toys and books. People were so generous.

Larissa and I worked on some special words and their meanings. While I felt overwhelmed when she called me Mommy, she also called her social worker Mommy. While she called Chuck, Daddy, she referred to the gentleman behind the McDonald's counter as Daddy. Often, she would say, "I miss you, Mommy." I would say, "Larissa, why do you miss me? I'm right here." We worked on those words for a long time.

The holiday season came upon us. We made plans to give thanks for Larissa and ring in the new year as a family. Thanksgiving was so special. We went around the table giving thanks with our family and friends. Everyone commented how thankful they were for knowing Larissa.

As we planned for Christmas and Chanukah the excitement in the household electrified us. We wanted to give this little girl a season to remember. We saw Santa and baked cookies, taught her about the Menorah and decorated the tree. We shopped and wrapped and counted the number of presents for Larissa daily. She couldn't believe all the presents!

Then, I got the call to go to court. I arrived at the courthouse ready to burst into tears. I met her social worker and the attorney. The attorney had never even met Larissa. I shared my biggest concern that she didn't know the real definition of Mom and Dad. It was important that she could learn it, and feel it, before it was too late.

In the courtroom, the attorney came close to delivering my words verbatim. I simply put the decision in God's hands. On one hand, I wanted to keep her forever. On the other hand, I knew her best interest was with Pam's family in Kentucky.

Larissa's biological mother sat on the witness stand. I wanted to run over and shake her and tell her to straighten up her priorities. I wanted to shout, "You can get so much satisfaction out of being a mom to this awesome child rather than living your current lifestyle choice." Larissa's mom didn't know me. But I already knew she preferred her lifestyle without her daughter.

"I understand, your Honor," she said as the judge spoke to her about terminating parental rights. "It's probably the best thing for Larissa."

The attorney asked the judge for Larissa's placement in Kentucky. In a split second, the judge agreed.

The ensuing void had already entered my heart. My family took the news in sadness as we prepared Larissa to return to

Kentucky. "I will miss you, Mommy," she said, using the words so appropriately.

We still planned to make Christmas and Chanukah magical with Larissa until her social worker called. "Her flight is on Christmas Eve. It was the cheapest unless we wait for the 21 days advance purchase," she said. I couldn't believe my ears. Evidently my heart couldn't believe it either. I cried at any moment of the day, thinking I had to say good-bye especially before we had the opportunity to celebrate the season.

When I told Larissa she would be leaving, she responded with an almost eerie acceptance, which I understood since leaving had happened many times for her. "Mommy, why are you so sad?" she asked.

"Because remember what I told you about missing you? It's going to happen, Larissa. I'm going to miss you."

I tried to make myself feel better by thinking she was getting the best holiday present ever - a new family and permanency.

I couldn't stand the thought that she'd think we gave her away. So I went to the bank and purchased a savings bond in Larissa's and my name. By this time, Pam and I had gained great respect for each other. It was easy to ask her to hold the savings bond sacred until Larissa was old enough to cash it. At that time, they could explain who I was and my family's role in her life.

I created a little scrapbook of the short time she was with us, expressing the extent she had touched our hearts. My family tearfully said good-bye. "I'll miss you, Larissa," I cried. "I'll miss you, too, Mommy, and now I know what miss means," she replied. Then she hugged each of the kids, Chuck, and Romeo.

A few days after she left us, I gave Larissa a call. "Hi Mommy. I got a new cat and I named it Romeo. Where's Daddy, Tanner, Addison and Jamie?"

Pam shared that everything was going well, saying "When Larissa says her prayers each night, she asks God to take care of each of you."

Sweet Larissa. How I hope we touched her heart and made a difference in her life as she did in ours. No doubt she'll learn the true meaning of mom and dad, and the meaning of sibling love with her new brothers in Kentucky.

My Children

Camp To Belong consumed my every waking moment. My kids rolled their eyes repeatedly and chuckled, "Who are you talking to now?" when I had conversations with myself driving the car. "Just singing!" I smiled, but they knew better.

My friends bellowed, "Helllooooo, where are you?" when they found me present in body but somewhere else in mind. I told them I was thinking about what they just said, but they knew better.

I laid wide-eyed in bed each night, visualizing each of our campers, wanting to tuck them into bed. When I finally fell asleep, I dreamed about this all-consuming labor of love.

I filled a pad of paper with cryptic notes as I rolled over during the night and reached to my bedside to record a thought. It wasn't unusual to get out of the shower dripping wet and grab that same pad to jot a note.

I followed my thought of the moment and turned "what ifs" into "gotta bes." Anything was possible, and I longed to make it probable in my mission to look out for the welfare of our kids.

I was the objective person in their lives, not only by listening but by hearing what they were saying and feeling. However, I wouldn't ever receive the award for Miss Feasibility. I wanted to be the old woman who lived in the shoe. I longed for all the kids to live in my home because I loved them, every one of them. Each had a spoken or unspoken potential inside. I knew my family would welcome them with open arms. I wanted the counselors to be my neighbors. After all, they believed in the purpose of Camp To Belong, and settled into the family with quick unselfishness and genuine camaraderie.

Chuck shook his head in all directions. He anticipated it was just a matter of time before my thoughts would spring into action and more footsteps would be heard in our home. My kids debated who would sleep where in the house. They were open to sharing their mom and I was proud of them. They lived Camp To Belong, too, willing to join some meetings, participate in promotions and experience Camp and its reunions. In the early days, they'd come to Camp for a day or two. Later, they'd spend the whole week.

Being consumed also meant being exhausted physically and mentally. Fighting the good fight by throwing it out to the universe was my style. When it failed to come back quickly, I wanted to ignite the fire of common sense. Brothers and sisters deserved to be together, just like my kids. Or, they deserved to have connection in an accountable manner, I fervently believed.

Sometimes the burden of momentum was too much to bear. On one given day, in one fleeting moment, I threw up my hands and sobbed, "I cannot do this anymore. I am quitting!"

My kids stared at me with wide eyes and mouths agape.

"But, Mom, you can't quit. You have to pass this down to us," retorted Tanner.

I was startled. Not until that moment did I realize the impact of Camp To Belong on my children. One can only model for them, sometimes never knowing if they truly understand the mission let alone believe in it. And at that moment, they left me no option to quit. My kids wanted a legacy.

Tanner has a mind like a fleeting bullet. We'd often call him Dennis the Menace. His quick wit, dimpled smile and "catch you off base" antics has us hugging him one moment and sending him to his room the next.

Standing in the kitchen one snowy morning, I raced to get everyone zipped up in their snowclothes to get them to school on time.

"Moooom, Moooooom, Mommmy," yelled Tanner pulling at my sleeve.

"Tanner, just wait one moment. There is only one of me," I responded in haste.

Without hesitation, he crossed his eyes, pointed at me with his finger waving side to side and said, "I see two of you."

Tanner is a ball of fire at Camp To Belong Summer Camp. From the early days when he came for a few hours to join the family, he made the rounds as if he was a business man working the room. He joins each activity with a zest for participation; his positive energy is contagious among those he touches with his jokes. An athlete with a deeply competitive nature, he stands back so others can shine and receive the rewards of attention and success. He is the master of the cannonball dive into the pool. He uses warp speed at the climbing wall. He is the first off the cliff jumping into the river. He arrives at breakfast with his hair tousled ready to take on the schedule of the day. His battery keeps running until his head hits the pillow each night. Called Mr. Smilearama, his spirit overflows.

Yet, as busy as Tanner is, all of a sudden when I least expect it, he is by my side with a bear hug. Tanner shows no fear. But he also doesn't hesitate to share his tears. At the camp-fires, he speaks about his new friends and his love for his own brother and sister. He cries when we have to leave. He openly talks about his friends at Camp To Belong, referring to them as his half brothers and sisters.

Jamie wrote: "Dear Counselors, you are going to have a great time at Camp To Belong."

I had created a monster. I watched Jamie and saw me. She had already figured out the method to the madness and initiated her role as my assistant.

"I'm going to help put together the letter for the counselors. Let me know when you're ready to assign the cabins and the families. That's my job," she explained.

Ownership is key to my daughter. She lives Camp To Belong and doesn't hesitate to remind me what has to be done for Camp. She does a remarkably thorough job of labeling items and stuffing welcome bags. There is so much she has learned just by watching. When I think she wasn't looking or listening, she is responding and answering. She has my check-list, always excited for the next Camp to start.

You can imagine how she felt when Andi and I decided to title her the Junior Ambassador. Quite honestly, she had no idea what that meant and couldn't even pronounce "ambassa-dor" when she started to tell people of her new role. As the honorary sister, Jamie could speak on behalf of all the siblings, reminding the counselors why they were coming to Camp and reminding me how to think like a child.

She feels a need to bring together squabbling girls who compete for each other's attention, and she plays the girlie girl games of whispering secrets to each other. She encourages the campers to love their brothers and sisters, and let each other off the hook when fingers of blame point too readily. She shares her personal possessions, not hesitating to give up a bottle of nail polish after a nighttime manicure and pedicure party.

Jamie befriends the kids as well as the counselors. By sending unexpected notes of love and necklace creations made for unsuspecting adults, she makes people feel special and reminds them about their impact on lives when they don't even know it.

She is a fish in the water and a master of the horseback ride. Her sibling pillow creations are well thought out. Even if she doesn't quite like her brothers at the moment, their pillow presentations shine with the foolishness of saying, "I really do like you, even though you drive me crazy." She knows she has talent as a dancer but, even when given the opportunity, she doesn't want to be the center of attention and won't take the stage unless she is with other campers. Jamie makes everyone feel special.

She won't hesitate to pull me to the side of the room and point out what would work better from a kid's point of view. At night, Jamie will find me in the darkness of the sky before going to her cabin to hug me goodnight and say, "Good job, Mom."

Addison is my quiet son. The oldest, he gets caught up between being a camper and being my son. At times, he wants to be a camper and then feels a need to be a counselor.

He watches many of the activities from the sidelines, yet participates when his name is called. He loves the rafting, although he turns up his nose at singing "Row Row Row Your Boat." He laughs with the kids at the carnival while holding cotton candy in one hand and a snow cone in the other. His quest to hit the target and send a counselor into the dunk tank is a highlight of that special evening. He knows he has to be a nice older brother to Tanner and Jamie, even if he has to pretend at times. He certainly doesn't have to pretend to enjoy the company of other campers.

It is common for Addison to put his arm around someone's shoulder and ask, "How are you doing?" at the moment that person needs a friend. When his arm isn't around a shoulder, one of the little kids is on his shoulders. They all love having rides with Addison. And when that arm comes around me with a "How are you doing, Mama?" I know that he knows I need some love and attention, too.

When the little kids speak to Addison, he kneels down to their height and gives them focused attention. When the big kids speak, Addison takes their lead.

Sure, behind the scenes and sometimes in front of the scenes, I have to go into "mother mode" to intercept sibling fights among my own kids. Sometimes, I have to reason with them to spend time together. After all, every other brother and sister has to be together at Camp.

"I know, Mom. Other brothers and sisters don't get to have time together like we do," will undoubtedly spill from the mouths of Addison, Tanner and Jamie at some point.

While Camp To Belong consumes me in many ways, it consumes my children in other ways. Their willingness to allow Andi and me to share our lives and their lives with others is an overwhelming compliment. And their support and participation in my vision demonstrates the true definition of "To Belong."

My Sister,
My Sibling Bond

The card I found was bittersweet. Bitter because of the sentiments inside, sweet because of the sentiments on the cover. I sent it to Andi.

"When I think of the closeness we share now...
I wish we would have known each other when we were kids."

I didn't know I had a sister until I was eight years old and she was nine and a half.

I didn't give her the time of day until I was in high school.

We didn't start our relationship until we were in our 20s.

Andi and I are best friends today.

"You were a pom pom girl?" I blurted out in skeptic laughter during a recent conversation.

"You were a cheerleader?" she laughed back with a brush-off wave.

To this day, we still learn things about each other and our separate childhood experiences.

Whether cheerleading or pom poms, Andi and I continue to be each other's greatest fans.

Sure, we are sorry we missed fighting over who was going to sit where in the car. I never got to borrow her favorite sweater. She didn't get to tell me about her first date. I never got to ask her for help with my homework. She didn't join me to blow out my candles on my birthday cake. I didn't celebrate her high school graduation.

However, we feel ecstatic that we made it as individuals and we share our sisterhood today!

Our mutual, unconditional acceptance of our individual memories in the past, lives of the present and dreams for the future stand as the solid foundation of our sisterhood.

Andi tells people she takes me everywhere in her heart. I often have to ask her where we went. She treats me as a celebrity and I can only hope she feels the tribute come back to her.

Andi is a clown. Really. At one of our Camp carnival events, she donned her clown costume. I didn't hesitate to have my face painted and walked around as her able-bodied balloon assistant. We weren't able to talk to each other in case the kids would recognize her behind the big red nose. But through our unspoken words, we were clearly having a blast. Laughter was the greatest medicine for all.

Indeed, Andi is the first person I go to when I need a laugh. Just the way she laughs makes me double over. The only one who can mimic my passion and cause me to laugh at myself, she's just downright silly at times. I embrace the opportunity to just let go.

Andi has taught me to celebrate the little things and I have taught her to work toward the big things. We are so honest with our feelings and always trust the roles of indecision, contradiction and devil's advocate. We know instinctively when to offer words, never empty words but meaningful ones. We also know when silence matters.

We stand beside each other as the "country mouse" and "city mouse."

We compliment each other all the time. When she straightened her curly hair, I had to take a double take at the photo she sent; I thought it was me. Others thought we were twins. I admire her fitness ethics and she applauds my big muscles, even when I can't see them. She's the first to say, "Good for you" or "I did something you would do." I'm the first to respond, "Back at ya" and "Thanks for the vote of confidence." We are proud of each other, always.

Sometimes in the heat of a Camp To Belong moment, one of us will shout, "Who thought of this anywise?" only to keep on keeping at what we were doing. When sharing Camp experiences, we read each other's minds, finish each other's sentences and honor the expertise of the roles we play at Camp and within our Camp To Belong operation.

Andi is the only person I could tell, "Leave me alone," then shake my head when she calls to say, "I'm leaving you alone."

Andi is my hero. She is a wonderful wife and awesome mother. A special educator for more than 25 years, she has taught people with special needs from kindergarten to adult. She volunteered during her college years at a residential camp designed for campers with cerebral palsy. She advocates for the rights for all individuals, believing no one is better than anyone else and that we all deserve the right to live our lives to our fullest potential. Along with teaching youth in the daytime, she also teaches evening classes to future special educators. And she advocates for my vision of Camp To Belong in honor of us.

There are no ego fights between Andi and me. Since the beginning of Camp To Belong, I've always spoken about the labor of love as *ours* and prefaced its passion with *we*. Often she has said, "This is your baby and stop saying we; you are doing it."

While this is my vision and my full-time career, I do see it and work it as "us." Her respect for my ownership and everyday responsibilities to build the organization inspires me to work harder for us.

We respect each other's individual passion, only to fully embrace the passions we share together. Some day, we'll add a special program for siblings with disabilities to Camp To Belong. Won't that be incredible?

We have been complimented greatly by the campers of Camp To Belong who admit that watching us get along encourages their relationships with their own siblings during their journey in the system and beyond. We are touched when they say, "If you have made it, we can too."

Often in a moment of pure emotion, I will say, "The truth is, we host Camp To Belong Summer Camp so we can spend a week together."

Andi loves to boast, "We get to share a bedroom. Thanks for coming to our party!"

Yes, Andi and I love a good party, whether over the phone or on a sisterhood excursion, whether over the Internet or through the mail. Our favorite party is a celebration with our Camp To Belong family.

Andi sent me a book *A Sister is Forever* from the Blue Mountain Arts Collection, edited by Gary Morris. In the inside cover she wrote:

"I love the fact that our relationship grows and grows. I love to love you and I love being loved by you. Our bond is unique. I will always love you unconditionally. Thanks for the laughs and the tears, the talks and the listening, and the just knowing. You are my best friend besides being my sister."

My five-foot stature is standing five stories high. May all the brothers and sisters of Camp To Belong, living in foster care or other out-of-home care as well as in cohesive families, celebrate their bond in the ways that keep Andi and I breathing. We are the cheerleaders and the pom pom squads for each other. Instead of taking our siblings for granted, we should always remember that our siblings always know us best…even when our childhood memories are missing. And, our relationships with our siblings will be the longest we have in our lifetimes. A sister and a brother are forever.

We are *real*. We belong. *Real* belonging.

Epilogue

I love Camp To Belong and everything our organization stands for. I live the mission during the day and sleep the mission during the night. I hold every camper, volunteer, care-giving team and contributor in highest regard and gratitude for believing in our vision to Give Siblings Their Right to Reunite®. The love is deep.

What can be the greatest love? The love of letting go. The vision includes a sprawling ranch in Colorado for a year-round haven of camps, reunions and meeting facilities with affiliate camps around the country and beyond. It also includes the celebration of the day that we can close the doors of Camp To Belong. On that day, I see all brothers and sisters in foster care or other out-of-home care living under the same roof or having an accountable, consistent connection plan in place.

Our quest is to dispense with labels and stereotypes. No longer called *foster kids*, our kids are *youth in care*. Perhaps it's a different kind of care from kids living with their biological families. However, they're in care, just the same. They are kids first and foremost.

I am humbled by the thought of being called a visionary. I believe that vision is not just about what we see; it's about using all our senses.

I can see it. A huge, colorful banner featuring *"Camp To Belong, Give Siblings Their Right to Reunite"*® waving over the entrance of our magical haven of brotherhood and sisterhood.

I can hear it. The outright jubilation of brothers and sisters excited about sharing a new camp adventure with their siblings. The inside silence of hesitation and skepticism about the adventure that lies before them as they reintroduce themselves to their own siblings.

I can smell it. The percolating coffee beckoning the counselors as they greet each day. The aroma of the crackling campfire that soothes all of us to bed each night.

I can touch it. The essence of a grand high five or a soft pat on the back. A child cuddled in my lap or hanging from a counselor like a jungle gym. The intangible touch of moving someone's spirit.

I can taste it. The sandy peanut butter and jelly sandwiches with the crust peeled away at lunchtime. The melting chocolate and gooey marshmallow oozing from the s'mores for an evening snack.

Common sense. It is common sense that brothers and sisters deserve the encouragement and opportunity to embrace their sibling bond.

Good sense. It makes good sense that the social service system and all supporters of our children put the sibling bond on top of their radar screens.

Bad sense. It makes bad sense to not fully acknowledge a relationship bond that lasts a lifetime.

Two cents. Of course, everyone wants to put their two cents in stating a myriad of objections: if, and, but, should, could, would, you'll never, you can't, you are crazy and then some.

Sense of humor. Having a sense of humor, justifies why we keep on keeping on.

Sense of belonging. A sense of belonging is undoubtedly what everyone wants in life. Thus, Camp To Belong.

Some applaud us for "finding" brothers and sisters. We don't "find" them. They usually know where their siblings are. Sometimes they even live in the same communities attending the same schools and religious institutions.

Some are more interested in those siblings who have been living separately for the longest periods of time. We feel one night of separation is too long.

Some wonder why we emphasize creating sibling childhood memories. It is a sure bet that these kids will journey out of foster care or other out-of-home care. We believe they deserve those memories to take with them.

Sure, brothers and sisters fight, argue and tease. In my home on any given day, one of my children wishes the other didn't exist. They may not know it now, but later they will recapture the memories of this sibling rivalry and embrace their relationship as mentors and best friends.

I am proud that while our quest has been to celebrate siblings in foster care and other out-of-home care, I am also inspired by many who've taken their sibling relationships to a new level of closeness without any attachments to the system. They say they can't imagine life without their siblings.

I have learned how many people are open to fostering and adopting sibling families and to connecting siblings in different combinations of out-of-home care, once they are aware of the needs.

I salute the reality that adoptive parents *do* honor the siblings they may not have adopted for one reason or another.

I am enamored at the resilient spirit of the teens who deserve to be embraced, even as adults, and welcomed into a permanent family. No teen should emancipate from the system without a family.

I applaud the insightful social workers and lawmakers who recognize that a permanent placement with siblings, or encouraging sibling relationships through an accountable visitation plan, is essential in establishing a bond that can be carried well beyond emancipation. Graduations, bringing friends home to visit, coming home for the holidays, weddings, births and deaths are all centered around family. It is our responsibility to give these children that bond with their siblings and a family they belong to in order to celebrate these milestones.

Sometimes our good intentions do backfire. Our campers are filled with love, sibling bonds and new friends all week at Camp. Then they separate, refreshed yet raw and depleted. They might "act out" when they get home. Sometimes the consequence of that behavior is the loss of their right to spend time with their siblings. Other times, this behavior clarifies the importance of the sibling bond and gives them their right to more time together.

Of course, these kids are tough. Everyone assumes they have baggage. Don't we all? It's up to us to lighten their loads. When you look them in the eyes and really mean it when you say, "How are you?" they become ever more trusting souls who yearn for reciprocal respect and understanding.

A camper kicked me once. But I just stood there, offering my hand to him. In moments, he was in my arms apologizing and wondering why I didn't send him home.

Another child had a big chip on her shoulder. She had no intention to spend any time with her brother. Then when he sang the song "Stand By Me," in front of the whole Camp To Belong family, she ran to nestle in his arms.

I wish, among all wishes, for a two-way mirror to be placed around Camp To Belong Summer Camp. The opportunity for the youth's entire support system to witness these exceptional kids individually, as siblings, and with other youth in foster care or other out-of-home care would undoubtedly change the face of the sibling system. They are so real. So precious. So full of potential. Yearning to hope. Deserving to belong.

As one of our campers said, "If I could change the name of Camp To Belong, I'd change it to Camp To Believe."

We all believe. Our Camp To Belong family lives the belief, the significance of the sibling bond, through our Power of the Ripple. Imagine yourself standing beside a still pond. You toss in a stone and peer at your reflection in the water. The rings spread out, and your thoughts of the moment and the reflection of their potential grow bigger and extend far beyond your imagination.

Every camper and volunteer at Camp To Belong believes and stands for what we call this Power of the Ripple. Once we acknowledge and honor the bond between siblings, more brothers and sisters will be able to share each other. It is the Power of the Ripple that allows us to Give Siblings Their Right to Reunite®.

I hope that youth currently separated will never miss out on the childhood adventures of every day life that Andi and I did.

I hope that those who wish to foster and adopt will embrace sibling families.

May Camp To Belong inspire you to never take your own siblings for granted.

Siblings, together, we *belong*.

It just makes *real* sense.

Comments or questions?
I'd love to hear from you:

Lynn Price
PO Box 261638
Highlands Ranch, CO 80163-1638
Lynn@camptobelong.org
To order additional copies of *REAL* BELONGING, visit
www.lynnprice.com

How Do I Love My Sister?

How do I love my sister?
It's hard for me to say.
I love her more than anything,
This love is here to stay.
Incredible is this person,
I know you will agree,
She makes my life complete,
This love she gives to me.

We can talk; we can walk.
We can laugh; we can cry.
These are some reasons,
These are just some reasons why

I admire her so much.
The love she gives to all,
No deed is too much for her,
No matter how big or small.

She has an insight into others,
That follows her every day,
She is a wonderful mother,
This I will always say.
When I am happy,
Who do I want to tell?
When I am sad or ill,
Her words make me well.

My sister is a part of me,
I carry her inside,
My love for her so strong,
Words cannot describe.
She has touched the hearts of many,
The memories and the song,
Thanks so much for everything...
Especially "Camp To Belong."

By - Andi Andree

Acknowledgements

When I set out to write this book, I yearned to share my story triumphantly and present a new definition of family that includes siblings as a vital component of the foundation. I found real belonging every step of the way, blessed with exceptional kindred spirits who listened intently and offered sincere acceptance and involvement.

Mary LoVerde, my mentor and a creative genius. You unselfishly unleash such significant insight and connections. With supreme honesty and commitment, you and your family validate me greatly, personally and professionally.

Lane Corday, Shelley Seidler, Darlene Superfine, Barb Meyer and Audee Whitman, my longest friendships. I will cherish our childhood and adult memories forever.

Amy McNulty, my first travel companion. From working on the Kibbutz to climbing to the top of Mount Sinai; to swimming in the Dead Sea; to living in the desert; to literally wailing at the Wailing Wall. Thank you for sharing some of the most defining moments in my life.

Teresa DeBroux, Heather McDowell, Jen Bronsdon, Amber Peterson, Patrick Harden, Jenn Reed, Darryl Weimer, Dan Farley, Bryan Cole, Randy Hubert, my dear friends. I appreciate your gracious contributions to my life and "*Real Belonging*."

LeAnn Thieman, my inspiration. Your precious gift of show, not tell, has taken my writing and speaking to a new plateau.

Craig Fuller, my captain. It's no wonder why you love sailing. You, the staff and members of the National Association of Chain Drug Stores have steered Camp To Belong beyond our Power of the Ripple into a magnificent tidal wave. Because of you, thousands of brothers and sisters celebrate their sibling connections in life impacting ways.

Scott Friedman, my torch. You have lit the way to the spirit of philanthropy, the expertise of speaking and the importance of faith. I am a stronger person because of you.

Bob Danzig, Jake Terpstra, Juanell Teague, Debbie Taylor, Kathy Barbell, Jim Bates, Tamra Cantore, Rick Schwartz, Lynn Wells, Candy Simunek, Patty Turim, Debbie DeMaria, Lynne Bee, Eileen Forlenza, Christine Testolini, Terry Prince, Juliann Jones, Penthea Burns, Cathy Roessler, Wendi Woodall, Karyn Schimmels, Connie Cass, Sandi Woods, Dick Milton and Kathleen Ohman; my amazing cheerleaders. I am humbled you have taken the jumps and flips and celebrated all the rah-rahs with me.

Linda Allard, Christall Rotta, Susan Burgstiner, Wanda Thomas, Leon Ireland, Peggy Leavitt, Darlene Chirico and Betsey Sheldon; my advocates. I value your vote of confidence for the method to the madness shown consistently since the beginning of Camp To Belong.

Stuart Fredlund and Judge Gerald Hardcastle, my colleagues. Just think, if you didn't say yes, Camp To Belong and I would not be where we are today. I am eternally grateful for your encouragement and respect.

Christopher Porter and Cory Scheer, my state of the art program directors. Through Anderson Camps and Noah's Ark Whitewater Rafting Co. & Adventure Program Ltd., for doing whatever it takes while working alongside each other to create a model of Camp To Belong Summer Camp affiliation.

Kirsten Marr and Barbara McNichol, my editors. Your literal words of wisdom have brought focus and integrity to my book.

Denise Gentilini and Lynette Prisner, the dynamic duo. Thanks for hanging on each and every, this and that, letter, word, sentence and paragraph, living each of them with me. I wouldn't be to the finish line without you.

All the journalists, photographers, behind the scenes media teams, and those who have nominated and selected me for prestigious awards; my messengers. You have honored me greatly by sharing my story and educating the world about the significance of sibling connection. Special recognition to: Oprah Winfrey and her colleagues at Harpo for the Angel Network Use Your Life Award, Joy Golliver of The St. Nicholas Foundation who introduced me to Robert Goodwin and his colleagues at The Points of Light Foundation for the President's Service Award, Mike Flatow of L'eggs Hosiery and his colleagues for the Women Who Shape Our World honor, Laura Wall Mansfield of Little Voice Productions and Sara Fogel and Hattie Kauffman of The CBS Morning Show for The American Hero honor, Parenting Magazine for honoring Andi and I as Parenting Leaders, Judy Dutton and her colleagues at Redbook for The Mothers and Shakers of the Year honor. Special recognition to: Heidi Collins, who created the first regional Emmy nominated video for Camp To Belong, formerly with KUSA, Denver and currently with CNN, Lou Ann Walker who wrote the article for Parade Magazine that catapulted Camp To Belong to international notoriety and Rebecca Cook and Ed Andrieski of Associated Press for spending an entire week at Summer Camp and living our story.

Volunteers, campers, contributors, supporters, former youth in care and Summer Camp affiliates; my Camp To Belong family. Thank you for believing in, and participating in, the quest to Give Siblings Their Right to Reunite®. I have learned so much from you. You are my heroes.

Jennifer, Zach, Logan and Lexis Feuer, my chosen kids. Your courage to reach out and let us in exudes faith in family.

Sisters of Sigma Delta Tau, my sisters of the yellow rose. You have no idea how incredibly special all of you are since our days of sisterhood in Champaign. Special thanks to: Nancy Daluga, Debbie Wolgast, Karen Zimbler, Sheri Tabloff, Debbi Weil, Betty Kolko, Barb Tatz, Diane Shapiro and Barbara Rosenberg. Thanks also to Lindsay Cutler, a recent Sig Delt graduate from Maryland.

My extended foster family, my family of acceptance. Thanks to all of you for always treating me as a real member of a family. Special gratitude to my cousins Audrey, Jeri, Jill and Steve and Aunt Charlotte and Uncle Murphy for being steadfast all along the way.

Bob, Ed, Matthew and Dan Andree; my brother-in-law and nephews. I so appreciate your acceptance of my relationship with Andi and your willingness to support our sister time and labor of love by jumping in the trenches at Summer Camp.

Andi Andree, my sister. Just when I think we are as close as we can be, we get closer. Our mutual admiration is more than anyone could ever imagine, let alone share. Thanks for letting me be me. Your unconditional love embraces me daily. Thanks for always being the one who makes me laugh, even at myself. Thanks for always believing in me, sis. Yes, you can introduce me as your little sister, anytime.

Chuck, my best friend. For recognizing my passion and trying to understand my starts and stops, my peaks and valleys, my challenges and my victories. For standing by my side through my life journey.

Addison, Tanner and Jamie, you are my life. Every moment of every day, I am so thankful and blessed for the love that we share. Thank you for letting me be the ever-present mother I never had, even liking me in front of your teenage friends, and loving each other even when you think you don't. Thank you for sharing me so willingly. You are my proudest legacy.

With thanks to all those who carried me through the system and beyond, too many to mention. You know you are my angels.

In memory of my parents, Jackie, Alex and Bernyce.

More About Lynn Price and Camp To Belong

Lynn Price, www.lynnprice.com

> Lynn Price, Professional speaker, child advocate, consultant and founder of Camp To Belong

Camp To Belong, www.camptobelong.org

> Camp To Belong is an international non-profit organization dedicated to reuniting brothers and sisters placed in separate foster homes, or other out-of-home care, for events of fun, emotional empowerment, sibling connection and lifetime memories.

Other related sites:

America's Promise, www.americaspromise.org

> Mobilizes people from every sector of American life to build the character and competence of our nation's youth by fulfilling five promises. Camp To Belong became an alliance partner in 2002.

Casey Family Programs, www.casey.org
>   Provides an array of services for children and youth, with foster care as its core.

Child Welfare League of America, www.cwla.org
>   Develops and promotes policies and programs to protect America's children and strengthen America's families

Children's Bureau, www.acf.dhhs.gov
>   Responsible for assisting States in the delivery of child welfare services and services designed to protect children and strengthen families.

Court Appointed Special Advocates, CASA, www.nationalcasa.org
>   Volunteer Court Appointed Special Advocates (CASA) are everyday people who are appointed by judges to advocate for the best interests of abused and neglected children

Foster Club, www.fosterclub.org
>   Provides foster children with a network that allows them to communicate with each other and provide them with education, motivation, and benefits that the foster care system does not usually provide.

National Foster Parent Association, www.nfpainc.org
Brings together foster parents, agency representatives and community people who wish to work together to improve the foster care system and enhance the lives of all children and families.

National Association of Social Workers,
www.naswfoundation.org
Works to enhance the professional growth and development of its members, to create and maintain professional standards, and to advance sound social policies.

National Association of Counsel for Children,
www.naccchildlaw.org
Provides training and technical assistance to attorneys and other professionals, serves as a public information and professional referral center, and engages in public policy and legislative advocacy

National Siblings Day, www.siblingsday.org
The purpose of Siblings Day, on April 10th, is to set aside a day to pay special tribute to honor our brothers and sisters who are living and memorialize those who have died. This day is set aside to remember the utmost importance of this relationship and to cherish, love and respect our brothers and sisters.

North American Council on Adoptable Children,
www.nacac.org

> Founded in 1974 by adoptive parents, the
> North American Council on Adoptable Chil-
> dren is committed to meeting the needs of
> waiting children and the families who adopt
> them

Oprah's Angel Network, www.oprah.com

> Oprah's Angel Network is a 501(C)(3) organi-
> zation supporting programs for women, chil-
> dren and families, educational programs, and
> health and human services

Points of Light Foundation, www.pointsoflight.org

> Engages more people more effectively in vol-
> unteer service to help solve serious social prob-
> lems. Honored Camp To Belong in 1998 with
> the President's Service Award